AF492328

Flourishing From Within

Reclaiming Who You Came to Be and the
Life That's Actually Yours

Tonille Miller

Elevate Press

Contents

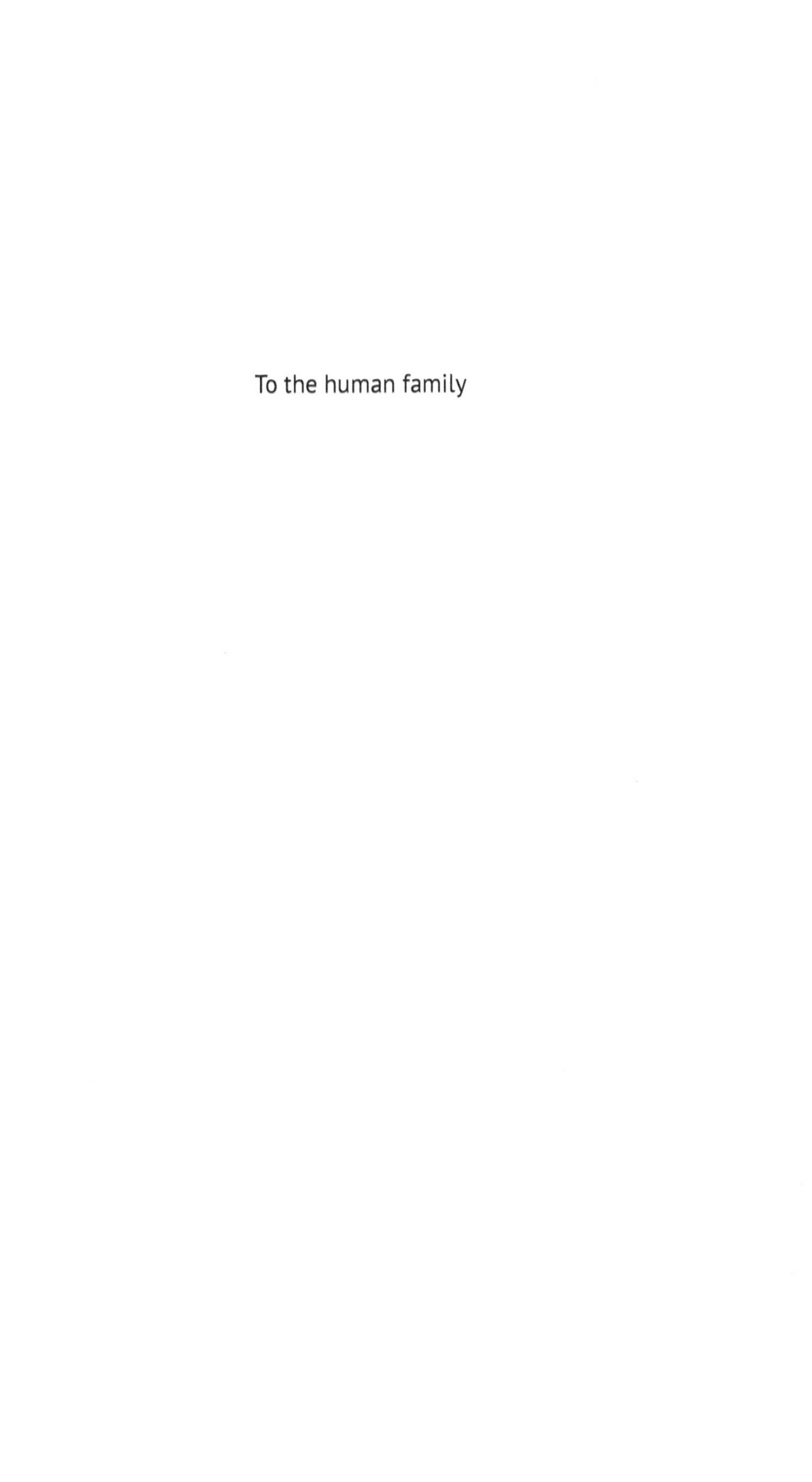

To the human family

Introduction

You know something is wrong.

Maybe you can't name it yet. Maybe you've been too busy to let yourself feel it. But in the quiet moments—the ones you spend scrolling at 2 a.m., sitting in traffic, or staring at your reflection in the bathroom mirror—it's there.

That whisper that asks: *Is this it? Is this all there is?*

I've heard that whisper more times than I can count. It finds me in corner offices and coffee shops. In quiet moments after a keynote. In late-night messages from people I've never met.

The voice on the other end is usually accomplished. Often impressive. Frequently responsible for leading hundreds or thousands of people. And yet the tone is almost always the same — a little quieter than expected, a little more searching.

They have the title. The salary. The reputation. The carefully constructed life. And somewhere beneath it all, a question they rarely say out loud.

Is this really all there is?

Not because they failed. Quite the opposite. They did what we're supposed to do. They checked the boxes. They followed the rules. They achieved things that should have made them happy.

And yet, successful on paper; hollow on the inside.

Let me tell you what I told them: *you're not broken. The game is.*

The Map You Never Drew

For too long, you've been optimizing for a definition of success that was never yours to begin with.

Most of us didn't draw the map. We inherited it. Somewhere along the way — through family expectations, cultural narratives, institutional rewards — we internalized a set of instructions about what a successful life is supposed to look like: Achieve. Advance. Accumulate. Repeat.

And to be clear, these things aren't inherently wrong. Achievement can be meaningful. Ambition can be beautiful.

But there's a quiet cost when the life you build is shaped more by conditioning than by conscious choice. You can end up highly optimized for a life that isn't fully yours.

This is the paradox of the high performer. The very qualities that helped you succeed — discipline, responsibility, perseverance, the ability to push through discomfort — can also keep you from questioning the script. You get good at performing. So good, that even you start believing the it.

You've been performing a version of yourself that was designed to earn approval, not to make you come alive. You've been building a life that looks good on the outside while slowly suffocating on the inside.

And the worst part? You've been blaming yourself for not being resilient enough, disciplined enough, or grateful enough to just be happy with what you have. But what if the problem isn't you?

The Truth They Don't Want You to Know

We are living through a crisis that goes far deeper than economics, politics, or public health. It's a crisis of the soul — a collective hemorrhaging of meaning, connection, and vitality that's leaving entire generations feeling lost, lonely, and desperate for something they can't quite name.

The numbers tell the story:

- 85% of execs report unhappiness despite professional success[1]

- Teen suicide attempts jumped 51% from 2019 to 2021[2]

- 77% of Americans experience regular burnout at work[3]

- 1 in 4 of us report feeling lonely, despite being more "connected" than ever[4]

What they don't tell you: your disconnection is a feature, not a bug. The anxiety you feel scrolling Instagram or Facebook? That's by design. The inadequacy that makes you buy things you don't need? That's the algorithm working.

The chronic stress that keeps you working 70-hour weeks while your life falls apart? That's the system optimizing — not for your wellbeing, but for your productivity.

You didn't accidentally become anxious, exhausted, and empty. You were systematically trained to feel this way because disconnected people are easier to control, easier to sell to, and easier to keep compliant.

Most of us have been living from the outside in without ever deciding to. We absorbed the scripts early from family, school, and culture about what a successful life looks like, what you should want, who you should become, how you should measure your own worth. And we went to work building exactly that, with impressive dedication.

The problem is that a life built from the outside in — constructed to satisfy external measures, earn approval, and perform belonging — will always feel hollow at the center. Because at the center, it's not actually you.

You can be universally liked and completely unseen. You can be objectively successful and quietly suffocating. You can build a remarkable life around a false version of yourself, and one day realize the mask doesn't fit.

That day tends to arrive uninvited. A milestone that doesn't move you the way it should have. A Sunday evening dread that no promotion can mitigate. A moment of stillness in which the question surfaces, unbidden and insistent: Who am I beneath all the performing?

Why Now

This question has always mattered. But it has never been more urgent.

We are living through a civilizational identity crisis hiding in plain sight. We built a world that is extraordinarily good at producing things and extraordinarily bad at producing thriving human beings.

We've perfected efficiency, productivity, and consumption while quietly neglecting what actually allows us to flourish.

And now, artificial intelligence is accelerating the reckoning.

For generations, we've tied our sense of self to what we do — to what we produce, contribute, and output. As machines begin outperforming us at those very functions, the question we've been deferring becomes unavoidable: Who are we when our work is no longer proof of our worth?

This is not a crisis of technology. It's a crisis of identity — one we've been building toward for decades.

The people who navigate it well aren't those with the best productivity systems or the most impressive résumés. They're the ones who've done the harder, quieter work of knowing themselves, and learning to live from the inside out.

Why This Book Exists

This book offers you a way out. Not through another productivity hack or manifestation formula. Not by "thinking positive" or working harder.

This is a field guide for reclaiming your life, and it begins with a truth most transformation books avoid: the systems are designed against you, and you still have agency. Both things are true. Denying either leaves you powerless.

Most transformation books pick a side. Either they blame you — just work harder, think more positively, optimize better — or they position you as helpless, a victim of forces beyond your control. Both are wrong, and both leave you stuck.

This book takes a different approach:

- It acknowledges the architecture working against you without letting you hide behind learned helplessness.

- It refuses to reduce human flourishing to achievement or happiness — you can check every box society told you to and still feel empty.

- It gives you a framework for reclaiming sovereignty without requiring you to opt out of reality.

Flourishing from within isn't about abandoning ambition. It's about ensuring that the life you're building is actually yours. And when that shift happens, success stops feeling like a performance, and starts feeling like an expression.

Underneath all the conditioning and noise, there's a version of you that knows exactly who you are and what you came here for. This book will help you remember.

The Journey Ahead

This book is a path, with each part building on the last, taking you from awareness to understanding to embodiment.

This book could have easily been 800 pages—there's a lifetime of research and frameworks here.

But you don't need more information. You're already drowning in it.

What you need is clarity, integration, and truth distilled to its essence. That's what this book offers, with curated rabbit holes throughout for when you want to dive deeper, and all of the research and thought leaders mentioned in the references.

Here's Where We're Going

PART I: The unveiling where you'll understand exactly how you got lost. How society, culture, family, and institutions systematically trained you to live from the outside in—to trust everyone except yourself, to value everything except what actually matters to you.

PART II: The discovery, where you'll peel back the layers of conditioning and operating system, until you reach the bedrock of who you actually are. You'll meet your True Self beneath the performance. You'll clarify your authentic values. You'll discover your purpose and why you're here. You'll learn to feed your soul.

PART III: The reclamation, where you'll learn to build a life from that foundation. Not someday. Not when conditions are perfect. Now. You'll build unshakeable self-worth, reclaim your inner authority, and integrate all of it into daily living.

By the end, you won't just understand yourself better. You'll know how to flourish as yourself—fully, unapologetically, without permission.

Who This Book Is For

This book is for you if you've achieved everything you thought would make you happy and still feel empty.

If you're exhausted from performing a version of yourself that isn't real — tired of living by someone else's definition of success, a stranger in your own life.

If you know something needs to change but have no idea where to start.

Or if you're finally ready to stop abandoning yourself just to keep the peace.

It's also for you if you're young and still figuring things out. The earlier you learn to know and trust yourself, the less life you'll spend living someone else's script.

Your Moment

Right now, you're standing at a threshold. Behind you is the life you've been performing — safe, predictable, and slowly hollowing you out.

Ahead is something uncertain but extraordinary: a life lived from the inside out, where meaning comes not from what you accumulate but from who you become.

A warning: this work will cost you. It will disrupt the comfortable lies you've built your life around. It will require you to disappoint people who prefer you compliant.

Some relationships won't survive your transformation.

Some old dreams will have to die before new ones can be born.

Some versions of yourself will have to be grieved.

And it will demand a courage you're not yet sure you have.

The promise: on the other side of that cost is a life that actually belongs to you. One where you wake up knowing what matters and have the courage to honor it. Where your days reflect your values instead of violating them. Where you are, finally and unapologetically, yourself.

Your soul has been whispering.

You've heard it in the dissatisfaction that won't go away — in the restlessness that keeps you scrolling at 2 a.m., in the tears that arrive without explanation, in the rage you can't quite name.

That whisper is your true self, calling you home.

This book is your map back.

The journey begins now.

Not when you're ready.

Not when conditions are perfect.

Now — because the life you were meant to live has been waiting for you all along.

Let's go!

PART 1 - How You Got Lost

Chapter 1

You're Not Broken. The Game Is

The Perfect Life You Never Wanted

Olivia stood in her perfect kitchen—with the marble countertops she'd agonized over for weeks, the built-in Sub-Zero that cost more than her first car, the six-burner Wolf range she never used, and couldn't remember the last time she'd felt anything.

She had it all. The 2.4-carat ring. The Ivy League degree. The Big Four consulting job pulling in six figures. Two kids, perfectly spaced. The body she'd starved herself for. The wedding that got the most likes.

She looked at her husband loading the dishwasher and realized she didn't know if she actually loved him or just loved that he checked all the boxes.

She looked at her children playing in the next room and felt crushing guilt. She loved them, of course. But had she actually wanted them? Or did she have them because that's what you do at thirty-one when you have the husband, the house, and the career on track?

The worst part? She couldn't tell anyone. Because how do you admit that you've built the exact life you were supposed to want, and it feels like wearing someone else's skin?

That Tuesday afternoon, standing in her perfect kitchen in her perfect life, she finally understood: She hadn't built this life. She'd been built by it.

Every choice—what to study, how to look, who to marry, what to want—had been made by a version of herself assembled from other people's expectations. Her parents' dreams. Society's standards. Instagram's algorithm.

The person everyone saw—the successful one, the pulled-together one, the one who 'had it all'—wasn't real. And the real her had been suffocated so slowly, so systematically, she hadn't even noticed she was gone.

Her husband felt it too. He was a VP by thirty-five. Corner office. Salary big enough to afford it all. He hadn't let himself go like other guys. Still fit. Still got the approving nods.

Driving home after another sixty-hour week, with another deal closed, he realized he couldn't remember the last time he'd felt anything besides tired. He didn't hate his job. He didn't hate his life. But he'd been sprinting so long, he'd forgotten to ask if it was even his race.

He pulled into the driveway of the house he'd bought to impress people he didn't even like, and it hit him: *I've spent my short time on this planet building someone else's life. And I have no idea what mine would even look like.*

But he couldn't say that. Men don't get to feel lost when they're winning. So he swallowed it, went inside, kissed his wife, and poured himself a drink. Like he did every night.

Your Story

If you're reading this, something brought you here. Something isn't working. And I'm guessing you're tired of pretending it is.

Read through this list and notice which ones land in your body:

- You feel hollow despite your achievements and accomplishments

- You're exhausted from performing

- You feel like a stranger to yourself

- You've lost track of what you want and value

- You're anxious all the time, and don't know why

- You resent the life you've built

- You can't remember the last time you felt truly alive

How many resonated?

Listen, You're not weak. You're not broken. You're not doing it wrong. You're navigating a world specifically designed to disconnect you from yourself, monetize your attention, and profit from your anxiety.

The hollowness? That's your soul rebelling against a life that doesn't fit who you ACTUALLY are.

The exhaustion? That's what happens when you spend years performing a version of yourself that isn't real.

The anxiety? That's your nervous system screaming that something is fundamentally wrong—not with you, but with how you're being forced to live.

Maybe you've had your own kitchen moment — the performance drops, the mask slips, and the truth lands: you've been on autopilot so long, you've forgotten there's a pilot.

If this is you, if any of this lands, I need you to hear something: You're not broken. The game is.

The Epidemic With No Name

This isn't just an economic, technological, or political moment. It's a crisis of meaning; a collective soul-sickness that no amount of optimization can cure:

- **We're lonelier than ever.** Nearly 25% of Americans are lonely[1]. We have 1,000s of online friends and no one to call at 3 a.m.

- **Meaning has evaporated.** A Harvard study found that 3 in 5 young adults reported having little to no purpose or meaning in their lives."[2]

- **Men are flailing.** Men have 4x higher suicide rates, 12x higher incarceration rates, 3x more likely to be addicted, homeless, and 1 in 3 under 30 are not in a relationship.[18]

- **The young are suffering most.** Suicide attempts among teen girls jumped 51% between 2019 and 2021."[3] The generation with the most comfort in history is the most anxious, depressed, and suicidal.

- **Burnout is the norm.** 77% of Americans report burnout at work as a regular feature of their lives.[4]

- **Even "success" rings hollow.** Only 18% of U.S. employees say they are very satisfied with their jobs, the lowest level ever recorded.[5]

I watched this truth destroy someone I knew.

John was a partner at one of Manhattan's most prestigious firms. Corner office on the 47th floor. Two kids at Dalton. Gorgeous homes in the city and the Hamptons. A LinkedIn profile that screamed: *This man has made it!*

On a Tuesday afternoon, he hung himself in the garage. His suicide note said: "I have everything, and I am nothing."

John had mastered the performance. The armor was so well-polished that no one could see the person diminishing underneath. The system rewarded that performance for thirty years. Right up until the moment it killed him.

These are symptoms of something systemic: a fundamental misalignment between how we're living and what humans actually need to thrive.

The Great Disconnection

You can have everything on paper and nothing that matters. Because you've lost the one relationship that determines everything else; the one with yourself.

We've become strangers to our own souls. We don't know who we are beneath the roles we perform or what we actually want versus what we've been told to want.

We don't know what makes us come alive because we've been too busy trying to stay alive in systems that demand we optimize, perform, and produce.

This disconnection manifests everywhere:

- **From our bodies:** You ignore hunger, override exhaustion, and power through pain. You haven't had a full night's sleep in years. Your body is trying to tell you something, but you're too busy to listen.

- **From our emotions:** You haven't cried in three years, but you tear up at dog food commercials. Your anger leaks out as sarcasm. Your joy has been replaced by the performance of enthusiasm.

- **From each other:** You have more ways to "connect" than ever—texts, emails, video calls, social media—yet genuine intimacy has become rare. You perform curated versions of yourself online while hiding your struggles, fears, and authentic needs.

- **From what's meaningful:** Without a sense of purpose beyond survival and consumption, life becomes a series of tasks to complete, goals to achieve, and distractions to consume.

- **From our inner guidance:** You've been trained to look outside yourself for answers. You've lost trust in your own knowing, intuition, your soul's compass. And without that internal reference point, you're lost.

Who Profits From Our Disconnection

The anxiety you feel scrolling social media? The inadequacy that makes you buy things you don't need? The chronic stress driving your 60-hour weeks while your life falls apart?

This isn't accidental. Millions of people didn't suddenly become weak, anxious, and depressed. This is the outcome of systems designed to extract value from your psychology, monetize your attention, and profit from your misery.

Big Tech didn't accidentally create a mental health crisis; they engineered it.

Instagram is engineered to make you feel inadequate, and it works. Internal Meta research found 32% of teen girls say it makes them feel worse about their bodies.[6] You see the highlight reel, feel insufficient, buy things, post for validation, and make someone else feel insufficient. A perpetual misery machine, minting money.

TikTok runs on the same mechanics as slot machines: Variable rewards, infinite scroll, content precision-targeted to your insecurities. Ninety-five minutes a day. Twenty-four days of your life every year. Gone.[7]

This isn't accidental. Your insecurity is their revenue stream:

- The average person now spends nearly half their waking hours on screens[8]

- Anxiety disorders among young adults increased 134% from 2008 to 2018[9]

- Depression rates among adolescents jumped 52% between 2005 and 2017[9]

I'm not condemning capitalism itself, which when done right, can be the most powerful engine for human flourishing ever created. What we have now isn't that. This is extractive capitalism that makes you sick, then sells you the medication to tolerate it. That's not a free market; it's a rigged game.

The Economic Drivers of Disconnection

The system keeps you trapped—starting with money. Financial precarity locks you into survival mode, where "finding yourself" feels like an indulgence you can't afford.

Since 1979, wages for the bottom 90% have grown just 26% while productivity rose 64%.[10] In that same period, housing costs climbed 118%, healthcare 601%, and college tuition 1,184%.[11] The math was never in your favor.

Then there's the insurance trap. 54% percent of Americans get their healthcare through their employer,[12] which means walking away from a job means losing coverage.

And student debt keeps millions more tethered — $1.8 trillion collectively, $37K on average, with a repayment timeline of 20 years.[13] It's hard to pursue your purpose when you're making student loan payments until you're 45.

So let's be clear about a few things.

You're not crazy for feeling that something's off. You're living inside a system designed to keep you anxious — because anxious people consume more.

You're not lazy for being exhausted; you're working harder than any generation before you for less security and less purchasing power.

And you're not broken for feeling empty despite your success. You've been chasing metrics designed to extract productivity, not create fulfillment.

The Invisible Prison

The most insidious part: We've normalized it. Anxiety, exhaustion, numbness, existential emptiness—this is just "how life is" for adults now.

We medicate the symptoms rather than questioning the system that produces them.

We blame ourselves for not being resilient enough, optimized enough, disciplined enough—as if the problem is us, not conditions never designed for human flourishing.

We live in an invisible prison and most of us don't even know we're trapped. The walls are made of expectations we've internalized, roles we perform automatically, beliefs we've never questioned, and constraints we've mistaken for reality.

Consider Your Typical Day

You wake up anxious, scrolling your phone before you're fully conscious, comparing yourself to curated realities.

You rush through breakfast — if you eat at all.

Back-to-back meetings, an avalanche of messages, lunch at your desk, barely tasting it.

You push through exhaustion because rest feels like weakness.

You come home depleted, collapse in front of a screen, and numb out.

Repeat. Day after day, year after year. Telling yourself it'll get better at the next milestone. But the next milestone never delivers the peace you're seeking.

Because the problem isn't your circumstances. The problem is you're living someone else's life while your own soul slowly suffocates.

The Crisis Beneath the Crisis

Here's what most people miss: the mental health epidemic, the loneliness crisis, the erosion of meaning—these are symptoms, not the disease.

The disease is a profound disconnection from our true nature. We're living from the *outside in* instead of the *inside out*.

We've outsourced our sense of self, our worth, our direction to external sources never meant to guide us. We've handed our power to systems and institutions that don't know us and can't see us.

We're trying to live authentic lives from inauthentic foundations. We're seeking fulfillment through paths designed for compliance. We're looking for meaning in a culture optimized for consumption and comparison.

It was never meant to work this way. You are not meant to measure your worth by productivity, your identity by achievement, or your success by others' approval. You are not meant to abandon yourself in pursuit of belonging.

You are meant to live from the inside out—from your essential nature, your authentic values, your soul's deepest knowing. But we've collectively forgotten how.

The Invitation

Whether you believe we've just entered the Age of Aquarius or not, it's clear we are watching the old world die in front of us. The evidence is everywhere.

Trust in government, media, and corporations has cratered.[14] Geopolitical alliances that defined the post-WWII order are fracturing, and climate disruption is reshaping where and how humans can live.[15]

Religious affiliation has declined dramatically—with the number of Americans identified as unaffiliated nearly doubling over the past 18 years.[16]

The great resignation revealed something profound: In 2023, nearly haff of workers had changed jobs or careers in the previous two years.[17] The top reasons? Lack of respect (57%), no advancement opportunities (63%), and burnout (48%).[17]

People are walking away from "stability" because stability without meaning is a slow death.

And let's be honest: That stability doesn't even exist anymore. Companies that promised security for decades now eliminate entire departments via Zoom. As I discussed in my first book, *The Flourishing Effect*[19], the social contract is broken. You can do everything "right" and still get a severance package and a generic "thank you for your service" email.

So people are asking: If stability is an illusion, why am I trading my life for it?

They're choosing meaning over the mirage of security. Purpose over pretending. A life that feels alive over a paycheck that funds a life they're too exhausted to live.

This isn't recklessness. It's realignment.

This transition, however painful, is not the end. It's evolutionary pressure pushing us to root our identity not in roles or output, but in something deeper—in presence, wellbeing, and alignment with our essential nature.

It's forcing us to ask questions we've been avoiding: *Who am I really? What do I actually want? Why am I here? What makes my life worth living?*

These aren't comfortable questions. They'll unravel the life you've carefully constructed if that life isn't actually yours. But they're also the questions that set you free.

We stand at a threshold. Behind us lies a world organized around external validation, productivity, and conformity.

Ahead lies something uncertain but extraordinary: a world where we reclaim our sovereignty, live from the inside out, and derive meaning from who we become, not what we accumulate.

But this new world won't arrive on its own. It requires something from us. It requires that we do the deep work of remembering who we are beneath the conditioning.

That we peel back the layers of "should" until we reach the bedrock of our authentic selves. That we dare to live from that place, even when it disappoints others, even when we're terrified.

The question before each of us is simple but profound: *Will I meet this moment consciously, or be swept away by it?*

The old world is ending. What emerges next depends entirely on whether we can rediscover a foundation for living that no technology can automate, no system can control, and no crisis can take from us.

That foundation exists. It's inside you. It always has been.

But first, you need to understand exactly how you lost touch with it—how the world systematically trained you to live from the outside in, to trust everyone except yourself, to value everything except what actually matters.

Because you can't reclaim what you don't know you lost. And you can't find your way home until you understand exactly how you got lost.

Chapter 2

The Programming You Never Agreed To

The Birthday Wish

Rebecca had an answer for everything. It's what made her exceptional, as a litigator, a mother of three, and the woman her friends called at midnight when their lives were falling apart.

She was the one who knew what to do. Always composed, competent, and five steps ahead.

When her husband asked over Tuesday takeout what she wanted for her 40th, she opened her mouth and nothing came out. "Oh, I've been too busy," she said, waving it off. "I haven't had time to think about it."

But later that night, she sat at the kitchen table reflecting. *What do I want? Not just for my birthday, for anything.*

She tried to name a single desire that was purely hers—not her children's needs, not her clients' demands, not her mother's expectations. Something that belonged to Rebecca alone.

The silence terrified her. She started making a list. Her morning routine: Optimized for the kids. Her wardrobe: Chosen for the courtroom. Her neighborhood: Picked for the right school district. Her friendships: Women who validated the life she was performing. Her marriage: Functional, respectful, but built entirely around logistics.

She looked at the page and realized she'd mapped a life where she appeared everywhere and existed nowhere. She hadn't made a decision based on what *she* wanted in so long that the muscle had atrophied.

She wasn't suppressing her desires; she'd lost access to them entirely like a language you stop speaking.

Three days later, she was in court delivering a closing argument when, midsentence, she stopped. Not a dramatic pause. A full stop. Her body refused to perform on command. The judge asked if she needed a moment. She heard herself say yes.

She walked into the hallway, leaned against the wall, and understood with terrifying clarity that this wasn't about a birthday or a closing argument. This was about a woman who had spent thirty-nine years becoming exactly what everyone needed her to be — and had done it so well that there was no one left inside to consult.

Rebecca's unraveling didn't happen because her life was falling apart. It happened because her life was working perfectly — for everyone except her.

Her story isn't unusual. It's epidemic. And what follows in this chapter is how it happens: The architecture of a world designed, layer by layer, to train you out of your own knowing and into dependence on external authority.

The Architecture of Outside In Living

Living from the outside in means measuring your worth by what others think, shaping your choices around what's expected, and abandoning your own knowing for a "conventional wisdom" that has nothing to do with your actual life.

This is the air we breathe. It's so pervasive, so normalized, most people don't even realize they're doing it:

The exec who worked 80 hour weeks for 20 years, missed her daughter's childhood, and stood at the top of the mountain only to find she'd climbed the wrong one.

The man who spent his life as the "strong, stoic provider" his father modeled, suppressing his emotions until they leak out as rage, depression, or a heart attack at 52.

The woman who can tell you exactly what every person in her life needs, wants, and fears — and has no idea how to answer that question about herself.

These aren't failures of character. They're symptoms of a system designed to keep us looking outward for answers that can only be found within.

How Sovereignty Gets Outsourced

It didn't happen overnight. Through generations, a thousand small mechanisms and well-intentioned impositions, we were trained out of our natural sovereignty and into profound dependence on external authority.

This wasn't malicious. Parents wanted to protect their children. Institutions sought to provide structure. Cultures developed norms to facilitate cooperation and survival.

But along the way, something essential was lost. We stopped asking: *What do I actually want? What feels true for me? What does my soul know that the world hasn't told me?*

Instead, we learned to ask: *What should I want? What will keep me safe, loved, employed, admired?*

We traded our inner compass for an external GPS programmed by forces that don't know us, can't see us, and often don't have our best interests at heart.

The loss of sovereignty happens in layers, through structures that shape us from birth.

The Family System: Where It All Begins

Your first experience of the world comes through your family. And while families can provide love and belonging, they also—often unconsciously—install the first programs that will run your life for decades.

By age seven, you've learned what emotions are acceptable and which must be hidden. You've absorbed beliefs about money, success, relationships, and worthiness that may have nothing to do with your actual nature. [1,2]

You've adopted roles—the achiever, the caretaker, the rebel, the peacemaker—that help the family system function, even if they suffocate your authentic self.

Most devastating, you learn through a thousand subtle interactions whether your authentic self is welcome in the world. If your natural personality or expression consistently meets disapproval, you learn to hide it.

You learn that love is conditional, belonging requires performance, and who you are isn't quite right. The message sinks in: *Don't be too much. Don't want too much. Don't shine too bright. Don't make waves.*

You learn to edit yourself before the world even gets a chance to see you.

Education: Standardizing the Soul

Then comes school, where the message is clear: there is a right way to be, think, learn, and succeed. And that way has been predetermined by people who don't know you and aren't interested in your talents and unique wiring.

The modern education system wasn't designed to cultivate souls. Its industrial-era roots prioritized producing compliant workers who could follow instructions, sit still, and perform standardized tasks without questioning.

Creativity, emotional intelligence, and self-discovery were never part of the blueprint. [3]

Creativity gets scheduled into forty-five-minute blocks. Curiosity gets punished if it veers off the curriculum. Natural rhythms get overridden by bells and rigid schedules. Comparison becomes constant—you're always being measured, ranked, graded, sorted.

External rewards like grades, gold stars, and rankings actually decrease intrinsic motivation and creativity.[4] Children naturally curious about a subject become disengaged once their performance is measured.

You learn that success means coloring inside the lines and giving the right answer—the one they want.

Religion: Outsourcing the Sacred

For many, organized religion adds another layer of external authority, positioning itself as the necessary mediator between you and the divine—telling you that you cannot be trusted to access sacred truth directly.

When you're taught you need an intermediary to access God, you learn something devastating: *You can't be trusted with your own soul.*

This is exactly why the Gnostic gospels were so threatening. These early Christian texts taught that spiritual truth is discovered within, through direct experiential knowledge. No obedience to institutions granting access required. No priests or bishops standing between you and the divine.

In the Gospel of Thomas, Jesus doesn't preach blind obedience to external authority. He says, "The kingdom of God is inside you and all around you."[5] The divine is already there. Your only work is removing the barriers that prevent you from experiencing it.

It's no surprise that teachings like these threatened institutional power. In the fourth century, church leaders declared them heretical and actively destroyed them.

They remained lost until 1945, when an Egyptian farmer unearthed them from a sealed jar hidden in the desert.[5,6]

Media: Manufacturing Desire and Identity

Media doesn't just reflect culture; it shapes it. It tells you who you should want to be, what you should want to have, and how you should want to look. Its model is to create artificial needs and then sells you solutions.

The average American is exposed to 4,000-10,000 ads daily.[7] By age 18, the average person has seen over 200,000 advertisements.[7]

This isn't passive exposure; it's psychological programming designed to manufacture dissatisfaction.

Media and advertising have grown exponentially more sophisticated and invasive in the digital age.

Social media has created an inescapable comparison trap. Spending just thirty minutes daily on it increases anxiety and depression risk by 13%.[8,9] You see someone's curated highlight reel and feel insufficient.

So you buy things, upgrade your appearance, and post seeking validation, which makes everyone else feel insufficient.

What makes this more than passive influence is the neuroscience behind it. Psychologists call it automatic goal contagion: when we observe others pursuing a goal — even briefly, even on a screen — our brains non-consciously activate that same goal as our own motivation.

Research by Henk Aarts and colleagues found this happens without awareness or intention; simply perceiving someone's behavior is enough to trigger pursuit of the same outcome.[17]

Media and advertising have weaponized this feature of human cognition at industrial scale.

You aren't just seeing an aspirational image and consciously deciding to want it.

Your brain is already adopting the goal before your rational mind has a chance to ask whether you actually want it — or whether it has anything to do with who you are.

This is why the exposure numbers matter so much. At 4,000–10,000 ads per day and over 200,000 by age 18, you have been shown other people's curated goals — their bodies, careers, lifestyles, relationships — hundreds of thousands of times.

Each exposure is a subtle goal-transfer. Multiply that by decades of social media, peer groups, and advertising, and what you experience as your ambitions may be less a reflection of your authentic self than a composite of everyone else's highlight reels.

The system doesn't just make you feel inadequate. It replaces your inner compass with someone else's destination.

Corporate Culture: Your Worth as Productivity

Next, there's the workplace, where your value gets reduced to output. You're only as good as your last quarter. Your worth is measured in metrics, KPIs, and your ability to contribute to shareholder returns.

An average of 68% of Americans identify primarily through their occupation.[10]

Losing a job triggers an identity crisis comparable to losing a loved one.

76% of Americans reported being stressed out by work to the point that it affects their mental health.[11]

You learn that productivity equals worth. That rest is laziness. That boundaries are a weakness. That your needs matter less than the company's needs.

Because your economic survival depends on employment, you comply. You mold yourself into whatever shape the job requires. You suppress your authentic self from 9 to 5. Or more realistically, from 7 to 7.

The message seals your fate: Your time, energy, and life force are commodities to be sold. Your value is what you produce, not who you are.

Captured Institutions: The Betrayal of Trust

The institutions we fund with our taxes and trust with our safety—the FDA, USDA, EPA, CDC—have been systematically captured by the industries they're supposed to regulate.

We assume if something's legal, it must be safe. But unfortunately, government approval often just means the lobbying was successful.

Just look at the numbers. The pharmaceutical industry spent a record $388 million lobbying the federal government in 2024 alone.[12]

And the revolving door between regulators and industry keeps spinning, with 38% of FDA appointees exiting to industry positions,[13] and 57% of FDA drug reviewers who left the agency went on to work for the companies they once regulated.[14]

The cycle: The food system is engineered to be addictive and unsatiating. You develop diabetes and other chronic conditions. You're prescribed drugs with side effects requiring more drugs. The root cause goes unaddressed because there's no profit in solving the problem.

Today, 88% of American adults are metabolically unhealthy[15] and 74% are overweight or obese.[16]

We trusted institutions to protect us. Instead, they protect corporate profit. We can no longer delegate responsibility for our health to systems that profit from our compliance. The trust was betrayed. Now, the vigilance is yours.

The Cumulative Cost

Individually, each of these forces might be manageable. But they don't operate in isolation. They reinforce each other in a system that surrounds you from birth to death, constantly training you to look outward for approval, meaning, and direction.

The result? A society full of people who:

- Have no idea who they really are or what they actually want because they've never been encouraged to ask

- Can't hear their own inner guidance because it's been drowned out by outside opinions

- Feel perpetually inadequate, measuring themselves against impossible, externally imposed standards

- Experience chronic anxiety and exhaustion because they're living lives that fundamentally don't fit

- Feel profoundly alone, because no one sees the real them

- Are sick, metabolically broken, chasing cravings engineered by systems profiting from their dysfunction

These are just some of the cost of outside in living.

This is what happens when we outsource our sovereignty to systems that were never designed to see us, know us, or care about our flourishing.

The Mechanisms of Control

This isn't conspiracy theory. It's basic economics and power dynamics. Systems perpetuate themselves, and systems that rely on conformity, consumption, and compliance have every incentive to keep people disconnected from their own authority.

Because sovereign people are harder to control, sell to, and keep compliant.

A person who knows themselves deeply, trusts their own knowing, and lives from their values is far less susceptible to manipulation.

They don't need products to feel complete. They won't work themselves to death for someone else's agenda, or abandon themselves for your approval.

Consider How The Incentives Align

Brands profit when you feel inadequate. If you felt completely satisfied, you wouldn't need most of what they're selling. But if you believe you're not attractive enough, successful enough, or productive enough, there's a product for that. An entire economy depends on your insecurity.

Institutions maintain power when you defer to authority. If you trusted your own judgment, you wouldn't need experts and gatekeepers to tell you what's right and true.

Employers benefit when your identity is tied to productivity. If your sense of worth depends on your output, you'll work longer hours, accept lower pay, and sacrifice more of your life than if you had a solid sense of inherent value.

Big Food and Big Pharma keep us in their sick flywheel. Food companies engineer "food-like" products that make us sick. Government agencies approve them because those agencies are funded by the industries they regulate. Then Big Pharma sells us medications to manage the chronic diseases created by the food supply. A perfect closed loop of profit extraction.

This doesn't require malicious intent. It's simply what happens when systems optimize for their own survival rather than human flourishing.

We're taught looking inward is selfish, following intuition is "woo-woo," questioning authority is dangerous, and that we have no sovereignty.

We're taught to be good citizens, good employees, good consumers. Compliant, productive, and predictable—everything except ourselves.

What We Lost

In outsourcing our sovereignty, we lost access to the very things that make life worth living:

Our self-connection. When you spend your life performing for others, you lose track of who you actually are underneath the performance.

Our joy. Real joy comes from alignment with your true nature and you can't access it while contorting yourself to fit external expectations.

Our relationships. You can't have genuine intimacy when you're wearing a mask. If you're performing, others can't actually see or love the real you.

Our power. When you don't trust yourself, you hand your authority to others and then resent them for the control you gave away.

Our vitality. We trusted institutions to protect our health. Instead, they protect corporate profit — leaving us too sick and exhausted to question the system.

Our purpose. Your unique purpose is encoded in your authentic nature. But when you're living someone else's life, you never discover what you came here to offer.

Our souls. Not literally; your soul can't be destroyed. But it can be buried so deeply under conditioning that you forget it's there. And in that forgetting, we become hollow. We check the boxes. We perform our roles. But we're not fully alive.

The Moment of Recognition

There comes a moment, sometimes gently, sometimes like a thunderclap, when we realize we've been living someone else's story. We wake up one morning, look around at our carefully constructed existence, and something deep inside whispers: *This isn't me.*

Maybe it hits during a panic attack. Or during a vacation you're "supposed" to be enjoying. Or at your promotion party, when you realize you don't want the job you just fought so hard to get.

Maybe it's quieter; a persistent sense of wrongness you can't name. An exhaustion that sleep doesn't fix. A numbness no amount of achievement or acquisition can penetrate.

It often arrives as crisis—depression, anxiety, illness, the dissolution of a relationship, or simply a breakdown of the structures that held everything together.

But this moment isn't a failure. It's an awakening. It's your soul tapping you on the shoulder and saying: *The life you're living doesn't fit who you actually are.* And you can't keep ignoring that without consequences.

The good news is that who you are at your core was never actually lost. It was buried, suppressed, trained out of you. But it's still there, waiting to be reclaimed.

You already have everything you need to live from the inside out. The knowing is in **you**. The guidance is in **you**. The truth is in **you**.

You don't need to acquire something new or become someone different.

You need to remember who you've always been underneath all the conditioning.

You need to peel back the layers of "should" and "supposed to" until you reach the bedrock of who you actually are.

You need to learn—or relearn—how to trust yourself more than you trust the crowd.

This isn't easy work. It requires courage to disappoint others in the service of your own alignment.

It takes discernment to distinguish between your authentic voice and your conditioned responses.

It demands radical honesty about what's true for you, even when that truth is inconvenient.

But the alternative—continuing to live from the outside in—is far more costly.

Because at the end of your life, you won't be asking whether you did what was expected. You'll be asking whether you did what was true for you. Whether you expressed who you actually were. Whether you lived your own life or spent it performing for approval.

The way back begins with a simple but revolutionary choice: to turn inward rather than outward. To listen to yourself more than you listen to the noise.

In the next chapter, we'll explore what it means to live from the inside out—to flourish on your own terms rather than by someone else's.

But first, you needed to understand how we got here. Because you can't dismantle what you can't see.

Chapter 3

You've Been Chasing the Wrong Things

Is Your Ladder Against The Wrong Wall?

David and James both have demanding jobs in tech. Both have two young kids. On paper, their lives look identical.

David wakes up at 5:30 am to a blaring alarm. He scrolls through work emails before his feet hit the floor, anxiety already building. He kisses his kids goodbye while checking Slack notifications.

His day is back-to-back meetings where he performs confidence he doesn't feel. He eats lunch at his desk, barely tasting the food. He stays late because everyone else does, because leaving at 5 pm looks like you're not committed.

He gets home after his kids are asleep. Again. His wife asks how his day was. "Fine," he says, pouring a scotch. He scrolls through his phone, numbing out, too depleted for actual conversation.

On Saturday morning, sharp pain radiates through his chest. He's at his desk—working through the weekend again—when his left arm goes numb. The ER doctors run tests. It's not a heart attack. Not yet. But his blood pressure is dangerously high. His cortisol levels are through the roof. The cardiologist uses words like "chronic stress" and "lifestyle intervention."

He's thirty-eight years old.

James wakes up at 6 am without an alarm. He gets a workout in and then sips his coffee while he makes pancakes with his kids, flour everywhere, laughter echoing through the kitchen.

His work is demanding, but he's set boundaries that would make David uncomfortable. No emails before 8 am or after 6 pm. He's turned down two promotions because they would have required managing people instead of doing the strategic work he loves. His colleagues think he's crazy.

But he leaves at 5 pm without guilt. He coaches his daughter's soccer team. He reads to his kids every night. When his wife asks about his day, he actually tells her—the frustrations, the wins, and the puzzles he can't wait to figure out the next day.

On Saturday morning, he's in the backyard building a treehouse with his son. His daughter hands them tools. His wife brings lemonade. The treehouse is crooked and probably violates several building codes. But it's perfect.

He's thirty-eight years old.

Same age. Same industry. Same family structure.

Completely different lives. David is successfully surviving. James is flourishing. And the difference has nothing to do with their external circumstances. It has everything to do with alignment.

David is living according to what he thinks he should do.

James is living according to what actually matters to him.

David optimized for the appearance of success.

James optimized for a life he doesn't need to escape from.

Twenty years from now, one of them will look back with gratitude. The other will look back with regret—if he makes it that long.

Here's what most people miss: The crisis isn't about your circumstances. It's about the relationship between your circumstances and your essential nature.

You can have a demanding tech job and feel alive if it aligns with your values and allows you to honor what matters most.

You can have the demanding tech job and feel like you're dying if you're betraying yourself to maintain it.

The question isn't "Should I have an ambitious career?" or "Should I quit my job and find balance?"

The question is: "Does this life—this specific life I'm living right now—allow me to become more fully myself, or does it require me to abandon who I am?"

That's what we're here to figure out. Not what success looks like. What flourishing actually means—for you, specifically.

Because you didn't come this far just to be successful. You didn't come here to collect the most things.

You came here to be alive.

Before we can understand what flourishing actually is, we need to expose what it isn't.

Most of us have been sold counterfeits; shiny substitutes that promise fulfillment but deliver only temporary satisfaction and long-term emptiness.

THE COUNTERFITS YOU'VE BEEN SOLD

The Happiness Trap

We've been taught to chase happiness as if it were life's ultimate prize.

But happiness is fleeting, surface-level—what the ancient Greeks called *Hedonia*. It's the pleasure of a delicious meal, a beautiful sunset, or the dopamine spike of a new purchase.

These moments are lovely. They're also not enough to build a life on.

Hedonia fades by design. The vacation ends. The new car becomes just your car within weeks. The achievement that felt monumental becomes just another line on your resume.

The high wears off, and you're left chasing the next hit, running on what psychologists call the "hedonic treadmill"—working harder to feel good, only to return to your baseline satisfaction every time. The treadmill never stops. The goalpost keeps moving. And you keep running.

You can experience happiness and still feel empty.

You can have the relationship, the career, the body, the impressive lifestyle—everything society promised would complete you—and still wake up with a gnawing sense that something fundamental is missing.

Because what's missing isn't another source of happiness. It's not a better vacation or a more impressive achievement.

What's missing is meaning, purpose, authenticity and alignment with your deepest nature.

What's missing is Eudaimonia—what Aristotle understood as the deepest form of human flourishing.

Not the temporary pleasure of getting what you want, but the profound satisfaction of becoming who you actually are.

Hedonia asks: What feels good right now?

Eudaimonia asks: What makes my life worth living?

Hedonia is the immediate gratification of sugar and likes.

Eudaimonia is waking up knowing your day and life matters.

Hedonia is the pig rolling in mud; it may feel good in the moment, but you're still a pig in mud.

Eudaimonia is the human who builds the farm, tends the land, feeds the community, and sits down at dinner tired but fulfilled, knowing the work mattered.

Hedonia leaves you empty the next morning.

Eudaimonia compounds into a life you're proud to have lived.

The Comfort Delusion

Our culture also sells us the idea that a good life is a comfortable life.

The goal, we're told, is to eliminate difficulty, avoid discomfort, and create conditions where everything is easy, convenient, and pleasant.

So we optimize for comfort: Climate controlled environments, frictionless transactions, swiping over dating, entertainment on demand, and food delivered to our door. Every possible inconvenience smoothed away.

But here's what we're discovering: Comfort doesn't produce flourishing. It produces fragility.[17,18,19]

When you avoid all discomfort, you don't build resilience. When you remove all challenges, you don't grow stronger; you atrophy. When you numb yourself to difficult emotions, you also numb yourself to the full spectrum of being alive.

The irony is that some of the most flourishing moments of your life probably involved discomfort:

- The challenge that stretched you beyond what you thought you could do.

- The difficult conversation that deepened a relationship.

- The creative project that frustrated you but ultimately produced something you're proud of.

- The physical training that was hard but made you feel capable and strong.

Comfort is seductive. But it's not the same as fulfillment.

You can be comfortable and completely asleep to the world of possibility...like a pig in mud.

The Approval Economy

And then there's life as a popularity contest. The one where your worth is measured by how many people like you, follow you, and approve of you.

This has been supercharged by social media, but it's always been with us.

The deep human need to belong has been weaponized into a never-ending performance where you're constantly auditioning for approval.

You curate your image. You post the highlights. You say what you think people want to hear. You present an acceptable version while hiding anything too weird, vulnerable, or real.

And it works—sort of.

You get the likes. The validation that temporarily soothes your anxiety about whether you matter. But you also get profound loneliness.

Because nobody actually knows you. They know the performance. The highlight reel.

And underneath, you're exhausted from constantly monitoring how you're being perceived, never quite knowing if people would still like you if they saw who you really are.

You can be universally liked and completely unseen.

What makes this more insidious than simple peer pressure is that you don't consciously choose to adopt other people's goals.

Research on automatic goal contagion pioneered by psychologist Henk Aarts and colleagues shows that when we observe someone else pursuing a goal, our brains automatically and non-consciously activate that same goal in ourselves, mimicking it as our own.[20]

This happens not just with people we admire, but with anyone we perceive as similar to us or whose behavior we observe repeatedly.[21]

Social media has turned this biological tendency into a 24/7 upload. You scroll past someone's fitness transformation, business launch, or curated life abroad and your brain silently files the goal. Not as "their goal," but as a felt pull, a vague dissatisfaction, a sense that you should be doing more.

A 2025 study in Cyberpsychology, Behavior, and Social Networking found that viewing social media posts can trigger automatic adoption of the goals reflected in that content, even without conscious intention to do so.[22]

The tragedy isn't that you wanted the wrong things. It's that you may never have wanted them at all. They were transmitted into you like a software update you didn't agree to install.

The lifestyle you're exhausted chasing, the milestone you feel behind on, the body or career or relationship you're quietly desperate for: Ask yourself where it came from. Was it born from your own deepest nature, your values, your unique experience of what makes life worth living? Or did you catch it from someone on a screen, in a boardroom, at a dinner party, from an ad algorithm that had already mapped your insecurities?

Goal contagion is the invisible mechanism behind a life that looks ambitious but feels hollow, because the goals were never yours to begin with.

The Wealth Illusion

First, let me say nothing is wrong with money. I LOVE money. Money matters. No one who has gone without it would tell you otherwise.

But it cannot purchase fulfillment — and once your basic needs are met, accumulating more of it without intention is just a socially acceptable way of staying lost.

Nobel Prize winner Daniel Kahneman found happiness rises with income only up to about $100,000 in today's dollars.[1,2]

Beyond that, more money barely moves the needle. A study of the Forbes 400 found that many were less happy than middle-income Americans, and none identified money as a major source of happiness.[3]

I saw this play out on Wall Street during my first months in New York. I watched a hot dog vendor laughing with his customers, fully present, enjoying the autumn sun.

Twenty feet away, a wealthy banker stood outside his firm's glass tower, screaming into his phone, cigarette shaking, face contorted with stress.

The vendor probably made just enough to cover rent. The banker likely had more money than he could spend in a lifetime. Yet their body language told a different story about who was actually wealthy.

Money boosts happiness when it's a result of meaningful work, but destroys it when it becomes the goal itself.

Let it serve your life — not become it.

The Achievement Mirage

And finally, there's the achievement model of a good life. This one is particularly insidious because it masquerades as purpose.

The logic goes: Set ambitious goals. Work hard. Achieve them. Feel successful. Repeat.

And when you accomplish something significant—the promotion, the degree, the recognition, the milestone—you do feel good....for a while.

But then the feeling fades, and you're left looking for the next mountain to climb, the next goal to achieve, the next way to prove your worth.

This is exhausting because achievement is never finished. There's always a higher position, bigger house, more impressive title. The goalpost keeps moving—an impossible target receding as you approach it.

It also doesn't tell you who you are. It tells you what you've done. And if your entire sense of self is built on accomplishment, you become terrified of failure, addicted to productivity, and unable to rest because rest feels like regression.

I see this constantly in high-achievers who've "made it" by every conventional standard. They have the credentials, the income, the respect. And they're miserable.

They climbed a ladder leaning against the wrong wall—achieving someone else's definition of success, now trapped in a life that looks right but feels wrong.

These are the counterfeits: Happiness without meaning, achievement without alignment, comfort without growth, wealth without purpose, approval without authenticity.

None of them is evil. Happiness, achievement, comfort, wealth, and belonging are all part of a good life.

But they're not the foundation. And when you mistake them for flourishing, you end up successful, comfortable, admired and....hollow.

So if flourishing isn't any of these things, what is it?

WHAT THE WISE HAVE ALWAYS KNOWN

For thousands of years, the wisest minds across cultures have circled the same question: What makes a good life? And despite their different contexts, languages, and frameworks, their answers keep pointing in the same direction.

Aristotle: Virtue and Meaning

2,400 years ago, Aristotle made a crucial distinction that we're still grappling with today. He separated Hedonia: fleeting pleasure, happiness, and enjoyment, from Eudaimonia.

Eudaimonia, as we just discussed, is often translated as "flourishing" or "the good life," but it's richer than that. It's a life lived according to virtue, a life of meaning and purpose, a life of actualizing your potential and expressing your highest capabilities.

For Aristotle, flourishing wasn't about feeling good in the moment. It was about developing excellence of character. He understood that humans aren't just pleasure-seeking machines, we're meaning-making beings.

Modern research validates this insight, consistently showing that people who pursue meaning and purpose report significantly higher life satisfaction than those who pursue pleasure alone. [4,5]

Even more striking: Pursuing eudaimonic goals such as personal growth, contribution, and meaningful relationships leads to better physical health, including lower inflammation and stronger immune function.[6,7] Pursuing hedonic goals shows no such benefits.

Carl Jung: Individuation

Carl Jung said, "The privilege of a lifetime is to become who you truly are."

He would have little patience for our modern obsession with happiness. For Jung, the goal of a human life is not to feel good; it is to become whole.

He called this process individuation: The lifelong journey of integrating the parts of yourself you've denied, hidden, or never been allowed to express. The ambitions you buried to please your parents. The anger you learned wasn't safe to show. The gifts you abandoned because they didn't pay.

Jung believed that everything you've rejected about yourself doesn't disappear — it goes underground, forming what he called the Shadow, where it quietly shapes your choices, your relationships, and your suffering.

Flourishing, in Jungian terms, means turning toward that darkness rather than running from it.

It means asking not just "what do I want?" but "what have I been afraid to become?" It means recognizing that the life you've been performing and the life you were meant to live are often mirror opposites.[16]

Jung famously wrote that until you make the unconscious conscious, it will direct your life and you will call it fate.

This is why so many people achieve everything they were supposed to want and still feel empty. They optimized the persona — the mask, while the soul went unfed.

For Jung, a flourishing life wasn't comfortable or frictionless. It was meaningful. And meaning, he believed, could only be found by becoming fully, courageously, authentically yourself.

Carl Rogers: Alignment

Psychologist, Carl Rogers described the "fully functioning person" as someone living in alignment with their authentic self rather than conforming to the "conditions of worth" imposed by others.

From childhood, we learn that love and acceptance are conditional. We're rewarded for being good, quiet, and successful. We learn to abandon our authentic selves in favor of acceptable versions to earn love and belonging.

The fully functioning person is someone who has broken free from this prison, trusts their own truth and lives from their authentic nature rather than performing for approval.

Research on self-congruence validates Rogers' theory, showing that people with high alignment between their authentic self and the self they present report 40% higher life satisfaction, significantly lower anxiety and depression, better relationships, and greater career satisfaction regardless of income.[8,9]

Flourishing is being true to yourself.

Viktor Frankl: Meaning

Austrian neurologist Viktor Frankl, stripped of everything in Nazi concentration camps—comfort, family, freedom, dignity, even his name—discovered that the one thing his captors couldn't touch was his ability to choose his attitude, to find meaning, to remain connected to his deepest values.

He wrote, "Everything can be taken from a man but one thing: The last of the human freedoms—to choose one's attitude in any given set of circumstances, to choose one's own way."[10]

Frankl flourished in a concentration camp not because he was happy—he wasn't—but because he maintained meaning and connection to his values even in hell.

Conversely, you can have everything—wealth, status, comfort, approval—and not be flourishing if you're living someone else's script, if your inner world is hollow despite the impressive exterior.

Flourishing isn't about what you have. It's about who you are and how aligned you are with that truth. And that can never be taken from you.

Abraham Maslow: Becoming

Psychologist Abraham Maslow gave us another framework for understanding human flourishing through his hierarchy of needs.

At the base are what he called deficiency needs: Safety, belonging, and esteem. These motivate us when they're absent.

But Maslow recognized that even when these needs are met, you can still feel unfulfilled.

There's another category he called "being needs." At the peak sat self-actualization: The need to become who you truly are, to express your unique potential, to live congruently with your deepest nature.

Maslow found that only 1-2% of the population achieves self-actualization, not because it's impossible, but because most people stop at meeting deficiency needs and never pursue being needs. [11,12]

Later, Maslow added an even higher level called self-transcendence.[13] This was the recognition that full flourishing involves connecting to something larger than yourself: peak experiences, service, and contribution.

The architecture of outside-in living keeps most people permanently anchored at the base — endlessly managing deficiency needs, never asking the more important questions: Who am I when nothing is missing and who can I become?

Martin Seligman: Living Fully

Psychologist Martin Seligman, widely regarded as the father of positive psychology, spent the first half of his career studying what makes people miserable — learned helplessness, depression, and pessimism — before arriving at a more radical question: "What actually makes people flourish?"

His answer, which he laid out in his 2011 book *Flourish*, went well beyond the conventional emphasis on happiness.

Seligman argued that wellbeing isn't a single thing you feel, but a constellation of elements you cultivate: positive emotion, deep engagement, meaningful relationships, a sense of purpose, and genuine accomplishment; what he called the PERMA model.[14]

Happiness, in his view, was too narrow and too fleeting a target.

Flourishing was the real goal. Not a permanent state of feeling good, but an ongoing process of living fully across multiple dimensions.

What made Seligman's framework so influential was its insistence that wellbeing could be studied, measured, and deliberately built, not just wished for. It moved the conversation from "how do we fix what's broken?" to "how do we help people thrive?"

Different thinkers. Different times. Different frameworks. But the same essential insight runs through all of them: Flourishing is not about comfort and what you accumulate. It's about who you become and how you experience life.

What Flourishing Actually Is

So let's be clear about what flourishing actually means—not as an abstract philosophical concept, but as a lived reality you can recognize and choose.

It's not about collecting titles, achievements, or possessions. It's about actualizing your potential and living from your authentic nature.

It's not about conforming to external standards. It's about discovering and expressing your unique essence.

It's not about fleeting moments of happiness. It's about a life of meaning, purpose, and continuous becoming.

Flourishing is the experience of living in alignment with your deepest, truest nature. It's what happens when who you are on the inside matches how you show up on the outside.

When your actions reflect your values. When your life feels like it fits you rather than like a costume you're wearing.

Flourishing has a distinct energetic signature you can feel in your bones.

It feels like flow. Not the absence of difficulty, but the sensation of moving *with* life rather than constantly battling against it. Even when things are hard, there's an underlying hum of *rightness*. You're challenged but not depleted.

It feels like aliveness. Colors are brighter. Food sings on your tongue. Conversations ignite something in you. You're achingly present rather than numbed out, fully engaged rather than sleepwalking.

It feels like energy. Not manic productivity, but deep, sustainable vitality—the kind that comes from living in alignment rather than fighting yourself. Rest actually restores you. Work that's aligned with your gifts energizes you even when it's demanding.

It feels like integrity. Your insides match your outsides. There's no gap between who you are and who you're pretending to be. You say what you think. How you act reflects your values. You're whole rather than fractured into performative "pick-me" pieces.

It feels like peace. Not the absence of challenge, but an unshakeable calmness underneath whatever storm is raging on the surface. You're anchored in bedrock. You know who you are and what you're capable of.

It feels like meaning. Your days matter; not because you're racking up impressive accomplishments (which you may be), but because you're living in service of something you actually give a damn about. Your work contributes to something larger than your ego.

This is not the same as happiness.

You can flourish and still experience sadness, anger, frustration, and fear. Flourishing includes the full range. Because when you're truly alive, you feel everything more deeply—the pain and the beauty, the grief and the joy.

Flourishing In Practice

The artist who works a day job but still makes time to create after work because making art is how her soul breathes.

The executive who turned down the promotion because it would require him to manage people instead of doing the strategic work he loves. He chose alignment over advancement because it felt right in his bones.

The mother who sets boundaries with her children—not because she doesn't love them, but because martyring herself doesn't serve anyone. She's discovering who she is beyond "mom," and she's a better mother for it.

The entrepreneur who co-founded a billion-dollar company then walked away because success without meaning felt empty. He went on to start a media company, merging his passion for storytelling with his commitment to human potential, creating content that helps millions develop the mindset to transform their lives.

The partner at a prestigious law firm who walked away after years of panic attacks and a marriage that existed only on paper. She moved to the country, opened a solo practice, and now works 30 hours a week. She knows her clients by name and has dinner with her husband every night. Her colleagues thought she lost her mind. She knows she found her life.

This is flourishing in practice. Not perfect, not effortless, but moving through your day and life, feeling aligned.

The Paradox

Here's what our comfort-obsessed culture doesn't tell you: flourishing often involves difficulty, challenge, and discomfort.

Working a second shift after your day job? That's hard. Turning down a promotion? That takes courage. Setting boundaries? That's terrifying.

Flourishing isn't the same as ease. Some of your most flourishing moments will be difficult. Training for a marathon is hard, but deeply fulfilling. Building a business is stressful, but exciting and expansive.

The difference between difficulty that depletes and difficulty that enriches is simple: Alignment.

When you're struggling toward something aligned with your values, the struggle feels meaningful. When you're grinding away at something that doesn't, no amount of success makes it feel worth it.

This is why someone volunteers for a stretch assignment can be flourishing while someone with a cushy, yet boring job feels hollow. The first is choosing difficulty in service of something meaningful. The second is succeeding at something they never wanted.

Flourishing includes meaningful challenge in the service of becoming.

Why Flourishing Must Come From Within

Here's what the self-help industry won't tell you: There is no magic formula for flourishing. No 5-step program. No hack. No one-size-fits-all blueprint.

Because flourishing must be authentic to who you actually are individually, it must come from within.

You are literally one of a kind. Your exact combination of DNA, life experiences, natural inclinations, gifts, and impact on the world, has never existed before and will never exist again.

This means your path to flourishing is also one of a kind.

What lights you up might bore someone else to tears. What drains you might energize them. What feels like integrity to you might feel like a compromise to someone else.

This is why following someone else's prescription for a good life—even if it worked beautifully for them—can lead you astray.

Your parents' vision for your life? It might be perfect for the child they imagined, but is it right for the human you actually are?

Your culture's definition of success? Does it align with your actual values and gifts?

The answer might be yes. But it also might be no. And the only way to know is to turn inward and ask yourself: *What's true for me?*

Not what sounds good. Not what looks impressive. Not what would make other people proud. What's actually, bone-deep true for you.

You don't need permission to live your own life. You don't need your parents to approve of your choices. You don't need your partner to understand your path. You don't need your colleagues to validate your decisions.

Great if they do, but their approval isn't required for you to live authentically.

The only permission you need, and approval that matters, is yours.

And that's terrifying. Because it means taking full responsibility for your life. It means risking disappointing people who expect you to stay the same.

But it's also the only path to flourishing. Because you cannot live someone else's dream and call it your own.

You can't flourish while abandoning yourself.

You can't thrive while performing someone else's script.

The life you're meant to live is waiting for you to claim it. But it requires you to turn inward first, to peel back the layers of expectation until you reach who you truly are.

The Bridge Forward

You now know what flourishing is, and why it must come from within—from your unique, authentic nature rather than any external formula.

But here's the problem: Most of us don't actually know who we are.

We've spent our entire lives being shaped by external forces—family expectations, cultural conditioning, educational systems, and media messages.

We've learned to perform, to adapt, to succeed according to someone else's metrics.

And in the process, we've lost touch with who we are underneath.

We don't know our authentic values because we've never separated them from those we've inherited. We don't know our natural gifts because we've been developing the skills that were rewarded.

We're strangers to ourselves. And you can't flourish from a self you don't know.

Before you can build a life from the inside out, you need to discover what's inside.

You need to peel back the layers of conditioning until you reach your essential nature.

You need to meet your True Self—perhaps for the first time.

In Part 2, we're going to do the deep excavation work:

First, we'll identify your unconscious patterns—the automatic responses and limiting beliefs running your life without permission.

Next, we'll help you discover your True Self beneath the conditioning.

Then, we'll clarify your real values; not the ones you think you should have, but the ones that actually guide you.

We'll uncover your unique purpose; the specific ways you're called to contribute to the world.

Finally, we'll explore what it actually means to meet your deepest needs.

This won't always be comfortable.

Meeting yourself honestly requires facing things you've been avoiding.

But there's no way around it; only through it.

Your True Self is waiting.

Let's go meet it.

PART 2 - Remember Who You Truly Are

Chapter 4

The You That Isn't You

She Disappeared in Plain Sight

Sarah's breakdown happened on the bathroom floor of her corner office, thirty seconds after closing the biggest deal of her career.

The CEO shook her hand. Her team was celebrating in the conference room. Her phone was buzzing with "congrats" from partners who doubted she'd pull it off.

She locked herself in the executive bathroom, slid down the cold tile wall, and felt nothing.

She thought, *If this is what winning feels like, what the fuck have I been playing for?*

Eighteen months of seventy-hour weeks. Cancelled vacations. Forgotten anniversaries. Missed her daughter's soccer finals. Her son asking why she was never home for dinner.

All of it supposedly worth it for this moment.

Sitting there, mascara running down her $800 blouse, she realized something that made her hands shake: If she could start over, she would not choose any of this.

She'd become so good at being what everyone needed that she'd vanished completely.

The scariest part? No one had noticed. Not even her.

She shared this story with me over lunch the following week.

The first thing she said: "I think I'm having a nervous breakdown, but I can't figure out why. I have everything I'm supposed to want."

That sentence captures the entire crisis in two words: *supposed to*.

According to whom? By what standard? Measured against what invisible rubric that everyone seems to know but nobody wrote down?

I've sat across from hundreds of Sarahs. Different names, different tax brackets, different breaking points.

But they all have the same look—that specific hollowness behind the eyes when they finally say what they've been hiding from everyone: *I have no idea who I am when I'm not performing.*

What It Looks Like In The Wild

Miles got the corner office at 43. But he felt absolutely nothing. "I thought I'd feel different up here," he told me. "Turns out the view from the top is just a better angle on the same emptiness."

Sam is already exhausted at 24. She's curated her Instagram so carefully that 2.1 million people think they know her. Yet even she has no idea who she actually is. She told me, "I became whoever the algorithm rewarded. Now I'm $95K in debt, selling a lifestyle I can't afford, performing joy I don't feel, for an audience that isn't real."

Kara did everything right. Valedictorian. Full ride to Yale. Big Four consulting. Perfect marriage. Two kids by 32. Then the 3 a.m. panic attacks started. "I kept thinking, this is what I wanted, right? But I couldn't remember actually wanting any of it. I just kept checking boxes someone else created."

These are different people with different definitions of "success." But underneath? The same crisis. They became so accomplished at being who they were "supposed" to be that they lost track of who they actually are.

Learn from what they discovered: You didn't lose yourself. You buried yourself. Layer by layer. Year by year. Under conditioning so thick you forgot there was ever anything underneath it.

This chapter is your excavation guide. We're going to peel back the layers—starting with the outermost conditioning (roles, rules, cultural programming) and work our way inward through your triggers, your patterns, your operating system—until we reach the bedrock of who you truly are.

By the end of this chapter, you'll understand exactly how you became a stranger to yourself.

Because you can't reclaim what you don't know you lost.

And you can't find your way home until you understand exactly how you got lost.

How You Became a Stranger to Yourself

You were born whole. You entered this world aligned with your True Self—pure, unfiltered, deeply connected to your essence.

You knew what brought you joy, what felt right in your body, what made you laugh until your belly hurt.

You expressed your needs without shame and experienced wonder as your natural state.

Then the world began to teach you who you were supposed to be. Family rules, cultural expectations, and social norms.

Each layer added weight, slowly reshaping your authenticity into something more "acceptable".

This is how the False Self gets built and most of us are still living from this place.

The deepest conditioning happens when you're most vulnerable; childhood, when your brain operates like a sponge, absorbing everything and questioning nothing.

85% of brain development occurs by age five.[1,2] Children's brains operate primarily in theta wave states (similar to hypnosis) from birth to age seven, making them extremely receptive to programming without critical filters.[3,4]

This is where you learned which parts of you were acceptable and which needed to be hidden.

Maybe you learned that anger wasn't allowed, so you became "the sweet one."

Maybe you learned that vulnerability was weakness, so you became "the strong one."

Maybe you learned that your needs were an inconvenience, so you became "the easy one."

These adaptations worked. They kept you safe, earned you love, and helped you navigate your family system. But they're still running your life decades later, long after the original threat has passed.

Invisible Constraints

When circus elephants are young, trainers tie them to a tree with a heavy rope. The baby elephant pulls and strains but can't break free. Eventually, it stops trying.

Years later, even when that elephant weighs 6,000 pounds and could easily snap the rope, it doesn't even try. A thin rope holds a massive animal—not through physical force, but through psychological conditioning.

You are the elephant. The constraints that shaped you in childhood—the emotional unavailability, the criticism, the conditional love, the impossible standards—are gone. But the belief in limitation has become internalized. You're free to escape, but you've forgotten how to pull.

The Roles You Didn't Audition For

To keep family systems functioning, families unconsciously assign roles: The comedian who eases tension, the achiever who brings pride, the rebel who takes the heat, the caretaker who fixes everything.

These roles become identities that follow us into adulthood, unless we recognize them and choose differently.

The "fixer" burns out trying to solve everyone's problems.

The "people-pleaser" loses themselves keeping everyone else happy.

The "perfectionist" never feels good enough.

The "rebel" exhausts themselves fighting, at all costs.

Childhood roles may have helped you survive. But they're limiting you now.

Ask yourself:

- What role am I still playing and who gave it to me?

- Do I still need it?

- What would I do differently if I stop playing this role?

Cultural Programming: Society Doubles Down

Society reinforces the programming with even more layers; telling you what success looks like (money, power, status), how to appear (thin, youthful, polished), and how to behave (agreeable, productive, always striving).

Research shows most people regularly compare themselves to others, with young adults doing so multiple times daily.[7,8,9]

Social media amplifies this exponentially—you're constantly comparing your behind-the-scenes reality to everyone else's highlight reel.

The programming is so pervasive, it's invisible.

You don't question why you feel anxious when not achieving, or judge your worth by your productivity.

These reactions feel natural because they've been reinforced thousands of times through subtle and overt messages about what it means to be "good," "successful," or "worthy."

The Courage to Disappoint

Breaking free from conditioning requires the courage to disappoint, the willingness to release who others expect you to be in favor of who you actually are. This isn't selfish. It's sacred. When you live from a place of authenticity, you give others permission to do the same.

Sometimes that awakening begins when you step outside your cultural echo chamber long enough to see it clearly.

I learned this after leaving the Midwest and gradually shedding what I now call "Minnesota Nice" — a chronic people-pleasing reflex that confuses politeness with connection and agreeableness with kindness.

For years, I said yes when I meant no. I accommodated others at my own expense. I swallowed my truth to keep the peace. I believed this made me a person who cared about others.

Since then, I've lived in places where people negotiate power openly, set boundaries without apology, and protect their energy as a matter of self-respect.

I realized my endless accommodating wasn't noble, it was self-abandonment dressed up as virtue. And the world didn't interpret it as kindness. It interpreted it as weakness.

I got burned. Hard. Many times. People recognized my agreeableness as an opening to exploit.

That was a hard awakening: Not to the world I wanted to exist, but to the world that actually does. A world where not everyone has good intentions. A world where being endlessly nice doesn't protect you; it makes you a target.

I had to shed an identity that once felt like me, to protect a truer self that deserved respect—one that refused to be walked on.

I had to practice saying no without elaborate explanations, setting boundaries without guilt, and disappointing people without taking responsibility for their emotions.

People may not understand. Family may feel threatened when you stop playing your assigned role. Friends may distance themselves when you no longer enable them.

The temporary friction is the price of freedom. And it's worth every awkward silence, every disappointed look, every relationship that cannot survive your evolution.

Because on the other side lies a life that actually belongs to you. One guided by inner wisdom rather than external programming. One that honors your unique blueprint instead of society's template.

I traded auto-agreeableness for self-respect and never looked back.

You can spend your life being who everyone else needs you to be, or you can disappoint some, and finally become yourself. The choice is yours.

Brules: Spot the Bullshit Rules

Mindvalley founder, Vishen Lakhiani, coined the term "Brules"—short for "bullshit rules"—outdated, limiting, or blindly accepted rules that society passes down to you.

They quietly shape your choices until you start asking: "Wait, who said this was the rule?"

Classic brules include "a college degree is required to be successful," "marriage and kids are essential milestones," "don't question authority," or "money is the root of all evil."

The Brule Buster Exercise

1. Identify a belief you've never questioned. What's something you believe that feels like "just the way it is?"

2. Ask these questions about the belief:

- **Where did it come from?** Parents? School? Religion? Media? Peer groups?

- **Is it based on truth, or just cultural convention?** Is there evidence that contradicts it? Are there thriving people who've done the opposite?

- **Does it serve my highest self?**

3. Write a new belief to replace the old programming.

- **Original brule:** *I must climb the corporate ladder to be successful.*

- **New conscious belief:** *I define success by the impact I create, the joy I feel, and the alignment between my actions and my values.*

- **Now you try:**___________________________

My first glimpse behind the veil came in a high school sociology class. The assignment was simple: Violate a folkway—an unwritten rule governing everyday behaviors.[28]

These aren't law, or even moral codes, just the invisible choreography of social life—face forward in an elevator, don't sit right next to a stranger when other seats are open on the subway, don't show up to dinner in your bikini.

That last one is exactly what my best friend and I decided to do. We wore our bikinis layered over our clothes to a restaurant — I still have the photos.

We were nervous walking in, hearts pounding, certain everyone would stare. They did, at first. But we held our composure, acted as though nothing was unusual, and ordered. And then, gradually, the stares faded. The world moved on. We didn't die — of embarrassment or otherwise.

It sounds minor, but that night cracked something open in me. It was the first time I understood, that most of the walls we bump up against are made of paper. They hold their shape only because everyone agrees to treat them as solid.

I've been testing that theory ever since and the world has proven to be far more malleable than most people realize.

You've seen how the conditioning gets built—layer by layer, role by role, brule by brule. Now comes the harder work: Not just recognizing the cage, but discovering who you are when you finally step outside it.

KNOW THYSELF

Aristotle believed knowing oneself was the beginning of all wisdom. Without self-knowledge, he argued, you are simply reacting to life rather than authoring it.

Ego: Your Survival Software

Just like your smartphone, you have an operating system running in the background, managing every function.

It's a network of beliefs, patterns, and programs installed over decades. Most of it runs completely beneath your conscious awareness, quietly determining how you interpret and respond to life.

Meet your ego: That part of you that's constantly judging, comparing, and defending.

Before you try to transcend it, understand: it's not evil. It's just outdated. It was designed to protect you in a world that felt dangerous. The problem is, it needs an update.

Your ego feeds on fear, scarcity, and separation. It thrives on identity, titles, achievements, and problems.[11,12]

It's the part of you that needs to be right, takes everything personally, and has a meltdown when plans change. It's also the part that oscillates between feeling superior and inferior to others. It's your inner critic, your perfectionist, your victim, your martyr. It's the mask you wear to be liked, even when that mask is suffocating you.

The goal isn't to kill your ego. It's to become aware of it, to recognize when it's driving, thank it for trying to protect you, and then guide it into the passenger seat as your True Self takes the wheel.

Shadow: Your Hidden Files

Carl Jung said, "When an inner situation is not made conscious, it happens outside as fate."

Think of your shadow as the repressed or disowned aspects of yourself you tucked away because they weren't acceptable to your family, culture, or the image you wanted to project.

These parts didn't disappear when you hid them. They just got buried in your subconscious, running background programs that create glitches in your system.

Carl Jung understood that these unconscious aspects must be integrated for true wholeness.[13,14]

Until you bring them into the light, they rule your reactions, showing up as triggers, projections, self-sabotage, and emotional overreactions that seem to come out of nowhere.

Shadow work is like debugging your personal software and shining light on what you've suppressed so you can transform it into power and wisdom.

Begin exploring your shadow by asking:

- What am I afraid people will discover about me?

- Which emotions am I least comfortable feeling or expressing?

- What did I have to do or be as a child to feel loved and accepted?

- What traits do I detest in others?

That last question is particularly revealing. The people who trigger you most intensely are often mirrors, reflecting qualities you've disowned in yourself.

The person whose confidence feels like arrogance might be showing you your own suppressed power. The individual whose emotional expression feels "too much" might be reflecting your own denied sensitivity.

Triggers: Your Emotional Tripwires

Triggers are seemingly small sparks that ignite reactions far bigger than the present moment warrants.[15] They're your psyche's way of saying, "This situation reminds me of an old wound that needs attention."

To detect them, notice where you overreact, where the same conflicts keep arising despite different people, and where your emotional response feels outsized for the situation.

The intensity is the clue—your psyche saying, "This isn't really about now. This is about then."

Early in my career, I worked under a female boss who seemed unable to stand up to a demanding male superior and I became hyperreactive and rebellious. At the time, I thought it was justified: *She's too weak to protect herself or her team.*

Once I dove into shadow work I discovered that this workplace dynamic was actually triggering the helplessness I felt as a child when my mother remarried an abusive man and seemed unable to protect my brother and me from his tyranny. These years later, I wasn't reacting to my boss. I was reacting to my stepfather through her.

When you don't recognize your triggers, they hijack you, pulling you into responses that belong to your past, not your present. But your triggers aren't obstacles to avoid; they're doorways to healing.

When you understand what flips your emotional switches, you can trace the reaction back to its roots, see the original wound clearly, and begin the healing work that frees you from living on emotional autopilot.

Trigger Awareness Practice

1. Notice when your emotional response feels outsized for the situation and pause.

2. Ask: "What's this really about? When have I felt this before?"

3. Trace the feeling back to its earliest memory.

4. Breathe compassion to both your past and present self.

5. Choose a response from who you are now, not who you had to be then.

Core Wounds: Familiar Foes

Core wounds are deep emotional injuries from childhood that shape how we see ourselves, others, and the world.[16]

They form when fundamental needs for safety, love, or belonging go unmet, creating beliefs like "I'm not worthy," "people will abandon me," or "the world isn't safe."

These wounds become invisible architects of our adult lives, creating patterns we repeat unconsciously.

My friend George unknowingly replayed the same pattern for 40 years until a therapist finally helped him see it.

He grew up watching his domineering mother berate and even physically strike his kind, stoic father. It broke his heart. He couldn't understand why his dad tolerated it.

That childhood wound created a devastating blind spot: George began subconsciously seeking the same dynamic, believing that's what love was.

As he remarried several times, the same pattern played out. Different names, same script. They'd treat him like a doormat, and he'd keep chasing them, trying to earn their love.

When his therapist connected the dots, George realized he was still the little boy who thought that was how people express love. It wasn't good, but it was familiar.

Attachment Styles: Your Relationship Blueprint

Your early caregivers set the blueprint for how you give and receive love.

These experiences created your attachment style: The unconscious template that shapes how you approach intimacy, trust, and connection.

Understanding your attachment style isn't about blame. It's about recognizing the patterns running your relationships so you can make conscious choices.[17,18,19,20]

The Four Attachment Styles

1. Secure: You trust others, connect with ease, and manage emotions well. You can be intimate without losing yourself and independent without cutting off.

2. Anxious: You crave connection, but fear abandonment. You need constant reassurance, overanalyze communications, and become a people pleaser in relationships.

3. Avoidant: You value independence and resist emotional closeness. You shut down when others want intimacy or dismiss your emotional needs.

4. Disorganized: You experience a push-pull dynamic, craving and fearing connection simultaneously. Love feels both desperately needed and dangerously threatening.

Reflection:

- How do you respond when someone you care about seems distant?

- Do you move toward others or away when stressed?

- What patterns repeat in your relationships?

Your attachment style isn't your destiny. With awareness and practice, you can develop more secure ways of relating.

To go deeper: Psychologist and relationship expert, Thais Gibson offers excellent resources on attachment styles, including a quiz to find yours, and ways to become more securely attached on her website www.personaldevelopmentschool.com.

Self-Talk: The Voice That Shapes Your Life

Self-talk is the running commentary in your head; the voice that narrates your experiences and tells you who you are.

Most people are completely unaware of this voice because it's so constant that it becomes background noise.

Why it matters: Your self-talk is the lens through which you experience reality and what guides your behavior.

Behavioral psychologists estimate that the majority of our self-talk is negative — actively critical or working against our own goals.[21,22]

Pause right now and notice the voice in your head. What is it saying? Is it kind or cruel? Would you speak to a friend the way you speak to yourself?

Most people, when they start paying attention, discover that their internal voice is relentlessly harsh.

They realize they've spent years accepting from themselves what they would never tolerate from anyone else — a relentless inner critic operating without oversight, without evidence, and without mercy.

The Voice That Became a Prison

In high school, I had a good friend who was brilliant, charismatic, and genuinely kind, but carried a gremlin in his head that told him he was worthless.

He believed he was a loser, a failure, fundamentally bad. As I watched him fall deeper into substances, depression, and isolation, I finally asked: "Why do you think of yourself this way?" He paused. "It's just what I thought the world thought of me."

The voice had been installed decades earlier. As a young boy with ADHD and a genius IQ, he was energetic and profoundly bored in traditional classrooms. He was labeled a troublemaker. During those same formative years, his father abused him, reinforcing the message: *You're the problem. You're broken.*

Those voices became his internal monologue. Even as others saw his potential, he never internalized the positive. That voice ruled his life and it eventually became a self-fulfilling prophecy.

The Voice That Became Wings

Reflecting now, I'm grateful for how my inner voice was shaped. It started when I was born with a physical handicap, and doctors told my mother I would never walk.

She refused to accept their diagnosis as destiny. She took me to every specialist she could find until she met an exceptional surgeon at the Mayo Clinic willing to attempt a new experimental procedure. It worked. After a year of surgeries and full lower-body casts, I learned to walk, dance, and run.

My mother's refusal to surrender became the foundation of my internal voice. My father reinforced it throughout my childhood with four simple words: *You can do it.* These became my wings; the unshakable belief that I could do anything I set my mind to.

I internalized those voices. They became my operating system. The result? I rarely experience fear, I don't doubt my worth, and I trust I can figure anything out.

Choose the Voice You Keep

The voice in your head isn't the truth. It's just the recording that played most often during your formative years.

My friend's voice told him he was worthless. Mine told me I was capable. Neither voice was objectively true; they were just the messages we absorbed. His voice became a prison. Mine became wings.

You can't choose the voice you were given, but you can choose the one you keep. If your internal monologue is harsh—if it tells you you're not enough, that you're broken—that's not your truth. That's just old programming.

You can rewrite it. Start by noticing. Pay attention to what you tell yourself in moments of struggle. Would you speak that way to someone you love? If not, why is it acceptable to speak that way to yourself?

Then practice installing a new voice: *I'm learning. I'm doing my best with what I have. I'm worthy of kindness, including my own.*

You cannot hate yourself into becoming someone you love. The voice in your head will shape your life. Make sure it serves your flourishing, not your destruction.

Personality

Your personality is the adaptive strategy you developed to navigate the world. It's not who you truly are, but how you learned to operate. Personality assessments are a valuable lens to help you see this more clearly.

Big Five (OCEAN)

One of the most respected, research-backed frameworks measures where you fall along five core dimensions:

- Openness (curiosity, imagination)

- Conscientiousness (organization, discipline)

- Extraversion (energy, sociability)

- Agreeableness (warmth, cooperation)

- Neuroticism (emotional sensitivity, reactivity)

The Big Five is grounded in decades of cross-cultural research.[26] It helps you understand your natural tendencies, so you can play to your strengths, anticipate your friction points, and grow with more self-awareness. Take the assessment at www.truity.com.

Myers-Briggs Type Indicator (MBTI)

The MBTI[27] sorts people into 16 personality types based on 4 dimensions:

- Extraversion vs. Introversion (where you draw energy)

- Sensing vs. Intuition (how you process information)

- Thinking vs. Feeling (how you make decisions)

- Judging vs. Perceiving (how you organize your life)

Take the assessment at: www.myersbriggs.org.

Enneagram

The Enneagram sorts people into 9 types based on what they most deeply seek. It goes underneath behavior to reveal the core wound driving it.

Type 1 (Perfectionist): To be right and good — driven by a deep fear of being corrupt or defective

Type 2 (Helper): To be loved and needed — driven by a fear of being unwanted or unworthy of love

Type 3 (Achiever): Success and recognition — driven by a fear of being worthless without achievement

Type 4 (Individualist): Authenticity and significance — driven by a fear of having no identity or personal meaning

Type 5 (Investigator): Knowledge and independence — driven by a fear of being helpless or incapable

Type 6 (Loyalist): Security and support — driven by a fear of being without guidance or protection

Type 7 (Enthusiast): Excitement and variety — driven by a fear of being trapped in pain or deprivation

Type 8 (Challenger): Control and autonomy — driven by a fear of being controlled or betrayed by others

Type 9 (Peacemaker): Harmony without conflict — driven by a fear of loss and separation

Your type reveals not just why you do what you do, but why you can't seem to stop — even when it isn't working. Discover yours at: www.enneagraminstitute.com.

Human Design

Human Design braids together astrology, the I Ching, Kabbalah, the chakra system, and quantum physics to reveal your unique energetic blueprint. While most personality systems describe who you are, Human Design shows you how you are designed to operate, and where you've been working against your own nature. It reveals:

- **How you're designed to make decisions.** Some people are built to respond in the moment, trusting their gut. Others need to sleep on it, and others need to talk it out.

- **Where you're most prone to conditioning.** Your chart shows your open centers; where you're most susceptible to absorbing other people's energy and expectations. These are often where outside-in living takes its deepest hold.

- **How to move through life with the least resistance.** Your "strategy" is the specific way you're designed to attract opportunities and create flow, instead of forcing, pushing, and willing things into existence through sheer effort. This can be revolutionary for high performers.

Get your free chart at www.myhumandesign.com. You'll need your birth date, exact birth time, and city.

The Bridge Forward

Now you understand how you became a stranger to yourself—how conditioning, roles, and programming installed an operating system that's been running your life without your permission.

You've identified the triggers, the patterns, the voices that have been driving your decisions. You've seen how your ego works, where your shadow hides, and what lenses you've been viewing reality through.

But understanding the architecture of who you've been acting as isn't the same as knowing who you actually are.

In the next chapter, you'll do what most people never do: Meet your True Self—perhaps for the first time.

Not the performed version, not the conditioned version, not the version that's been trying so hard to be acceptable. The real you; the one that's been waiting beneath this entire time.

Chapter 5

Meet Your True Self

Who Are You Really?

Emilie found the photo while renovating her house during the pandemic—a Polaroid that must have slipped behind a baseboard years ago.

In it, she's seven years old, standing in the backyard, hands on her hips, wearing a cape she'd fashioned from a bedsheet.

She's grinning at the camera with the kind of confidence that only exists before the world teaches you to doubt yourself. Her hair is a tangled mess. Her knees are scraped and dirty.

And she clearly doesn't give a damn.

Emilie sat on the floor surrounded by debris and stared at that photo for twenty minutes.

The girl in that picture knew exactly who she was. She hadn't learned yet that her laugh was too loud. That her ideas were too big. That her energy was too much.

She woke up every morning knowing what she wanted to do that day—not what she "should" do, but what lit her up from the inside.

She expressed her opinions without apologizing. She had boundaries she enforced without guilt. She took up space without asking permission. She was whole, sovereign, and utterly, unapologetically herself.

Somewhere between that photo and the 43 year-old woman sitting on the floor holding it, Emilie had lost her completely.

She framed that photo. Put it on her desk where she'd see it every day.

For the first time in decades, she could feel that girl again. Beneath all the layers of conditioning. All the "shoulds" and "supposed tos." All the carefully constructed armor she'd built to survive.

She was still there. Quieter now. Buried deeper. But alive.

And she was pissed!

You Weren't Born Performing

You weren't born people-pleasing, playing small, second-guessing yourself, or organizing your life around external validation.

You were born sovereign. You knew what you wanted. You knew what you felt. You knew what was true for you without needing confirmation.

You had an inner compass that pointed true north, and you trusted it without question.

Then the world taught you not to. And you spent the next few decades trying to figure out who you were supposed to be—instead of remembering who you already were.

Reclaiming your life means finding your way back to yourself. Not to childhood, but to the essence of who you were before the conditioning. Before the performance. Before you learned that being yourself wasn't safe. Wasn't enough. Wasn't okay.

The version of you that knew what you wanted without polling the room. The version that felt your feelings without apologizing. The version that took up space because it never occurred to you that you shouldn't.

Who You Actually Are

We weren't meant to forget who we are or why we're here.

We weren't born to "spend our lives working jobs we hate to buy things we don't need, to impress people we don't like", as Chuck Palahniuk wrote in *Fight Club*, or to live lives of quiet desperation written about by Thoreau.[1]

We weren't meant to sleepwalk through curated, performative lives, measuring worth in metrics and milestones, desperately trying to earn "enough-ness".

We're here to embody our unique blueprint. To wake up. To remember. To become vessels for something greater than the ego-based avatars society insists we are.

So if you aren't who society tells you to be, who are you?

You Are a Miracle

The odds of your existence? One in 400 trillion.[2,3] Your body? 97% stardust, forged in ancient supernovae.[4] No one else carries your DNA, your fingerprints, your singular constellation of experiences, desires, and inclinations.[5]

This isn't "woo-woo". It's physics, biology, and math screaming a truth we've learned to ignore: We are each a walking miracle.

You Are Made of Stars

Literally. Our bodies are composed of elements like carbon, oxygen, and nitrogen—forged in the hearts of dying stars and scattered through the cosmos.

We are stardust with a nervous system. We are the universe becoming aware of itself.

You Are Energy

Einstein's famous equation, $E = mc^2$, tells us that matter and energy are interchangeable.[6]

At the quantum level, everything is energy, including you. You are not a solid thing but a dynamic field of vibrating energy. Your emotions, thoughts, and presence all carry an energetic vibration.

You Are a Portal

You're not just here to grind, scroll, or survive. You are a portal; a living vessel for the Divine intelligence that flows through everything.[9]

You don't have to create the light. You just have to let it through. When you strip away ego, fear, and conditioning, you become a clear channel for love, truth, creativity, healing, and purpose to shine through.

You Are Part of the Divine Orchestra

There are no spare parts in the universe. You are a note in the symphony of existence — a unique vibration, a singular frequency that has never existed before and will never exist again.

You are not here to follow someone else's script. You're here to live your own sacred, messy, irreplaceable story.

Some of us are meant to heal. Others to lead, to create beauty, to disrupt what has calcified, to awaken what has gone numb. None of these callings is more important than another. All of them are necessary.

A tree doesn't ask permission to grow tall. A flower doesn't dim its color for fear of being too much. The sun doesn't negotiate its brightness to make others comfortable. Nature doesn't perform itself. It simply is itself, completely, without apology.

We were made from the same source. The same permission applies.

You Are a Fractal of God

As spiritual thought leader, Cathy Heller beautifully expresses, "You are a masterpiece because you are a piece of the Master." Across centuries and cultures, deep spiritual traditions have pointed to the same truth: The light within us is identical to the light of God.

Divinity isn't somewhere out there. It's in here. You are not just made by the Divine; you are of It. Like a hologram where each fragment contains the whole image, you are a fractal expression of infinite consciousness.

You Are a Spiritual Being

As priest, scientist, and philosopher Pierre Teilhard de Chardin said, "We are not human beings having a spiritual experience; we are spiritual beings having a human experience."[7]

There is infinitely more to you than your resume, your roles, or the temporary meat suit you inhabit.

Beneath the surface of personality and circumstance lives an essential lifeforce—call it soul, spirit, essence, or pure consciousness. This is the deepest, truest part of you.

Most remarkably, your spiritual essence is utterly, uniquely you.

When you know yourself as primarily spiritual rather than material, you stop looking for validation from a mundane world that was never designed to complete you.

You Are the Human Expression of Your Soul

Your soul is eternal, timeless, infinite. But your True Self? That's how your soul expresses itself in this lifetime, through this body, in this moment in history.

Your True Self emerges when you shed the layers of societal conditioning, inherited beliefs, and fear-based patterns that cover your essential nature.

When your actions align with your soul's intentions, when your choices reflect your deepest values rather than external expectations, you're expressing your True Self.

Your soul naturally expresses itself through you. It flows through emotions that reflect your inner truth, manifests in acts of love, shines through creative pursuits, and speaks through your passions.

Your dreams, your natural talents, your fascination with certain subjects—these are breadcrumbs leading you back to who you really are.

When you honor and express your True Self, you give the world a gift that only you can give.

What If Your Remembered

What if you knew—not just as a comforting idea, but as a bone-deep truth—that you are a miracle and are here for a reason? Not an accident. Not someone who has to contort themselves to be worthy.

What if you trusted that the path in front of you was handcrafted for your becoming—the twists, the setbacks, the wins, the lessons?

Imagine how it would feel to shine your light without apology—no shrinking to keep others comfortable, no overperforming to prove your worth, no outsourcing your power to someone else's approval.

The mission you came here to accomplish lives in your marrow. It calls to you in the quiet moments. And it will keep calling until you answer.

So what if today, instead of questioning your worth or waiting for permission, you simply remembered: You are here on purpose. Your light is needed. The world doesn't benefit from you playing small.

What Is the True Self?

The True Self is not spiritual fluff. Rooted in the Greek word psyche—meaning soul—it's the essence of you: Your deepest values, passions, purpose, innate wisdom, and cosmic connection.

It's what remains when you strip away society's scripts, the ego's noise, and the chains of fear.

Carl Jung described the soul as an inner witness that knows you better than you know yourself, quietly nudging you toward truth.[10]

The True Self is how your soul shows up in your human experience, in this lifetime, with these specific gifts and assignments.

In plain English? The True Self is your purest, most authentic "you"—unedited, unperformed, undiluted by conditioning.

When your choices reflect your soul's intentions, you become your True Self. Life suddenly feels spacious, light, and aligned. The world's noise fades, and you hear your intuition clearly. Decisions flow naturally.

Spiritual teacher Gary Zukav describes this alignment as when your personality becomes a servant to your soul. And that's when you step into your authentic power.[11]

Your Essence

Your True Self isn't something you have to hunt down; it's been inside you all along. Your job? Turn off the noise until only the truth remains.

Ways to do it:

- **Get quiet.** Stillness isn't a luxury; it's your lifeline. Meditation, nature, breathwork—whatever shuts down the mental circus.

- **Recall what used to light you up.** Moments of joy and feeling fully alive is your soul is waving at you.

- **Feel your feelings.** Emotions are intel, not obstacles. Your soul communicates through sensation.

- **Be alone without feeling lonely.** Solitude detoxes external noise and lets your inner voice ring clear.

- **Move your body.** Dance, stretch, walk, breathe. Your truth lives in your vessel.

- **Create for the hell of it.** Paint, write, sing, make something just because.

Your Inner GPS

We're born connected to our inner knowing—until we're trained out of it.

Systems and external authorities have convinced us that someone else knows better. Why? Because disconnected people are easier to manipulate, control, and sell to.

Intuition is the raw, immediate knowing that rises from your True Self, often with no trail of logic. It's quick, instinctive—a gut nudge or a quiet yes or no.

Your inner wisdom is a built-in GPS: Subtle, but unfailingly reliable. Ignore it, and the external world takes the wheel, resulting in confusion, fragmentation and drifting.

Reclaiming your True Self means trusting your soul's quiet wisdom over the ego's constant chatter. But you can't hear that wisdom if you're always busy, consuming content, never slowing down.

Try these:

The decision body scan: When facing a decision, sit quietly. Close your eyes. Think about Option A and notice what happens in your body. Does your chest tighten or open? Does your breathing get shallow or deep? Does your stomach clench or relax? Now clear that and think about Option B. Notice your body's response again.

Your body knows before your mind does. Expansion, opening, deeper breath—that's your yes. Contraction, tightness, shallow breath—that's your no.

The daily pause: Set a timer for 5 minutes. Sit in silence with no distractions and simply ask, *what do I need to hear right now?* Then listen with your whole being. The first few times, you might hear nothing but mental chatter. That's normal. Keep showing up.

Your intuition is always speaking. You're just learning to listen again.

The Bridge Forward

Now you've met your True Self. Not the performed or conditioned version, but the essence of who you are.

But knowing it isn't the same as building a life from it. The work now is organizing your life around that truth.

And that starts with getting crystal clear on what actually matters to you; not what you think should matter, but what your soul genuinely values.

In the next chapter, we'll identify your authentic values—the non-negotiables that, when honored, make you feel alive, and when betrayed, make you feel like you're slowly dying inside.

This is where your True Self becomes a practical compass for every decision you make.

Chapter 6

What Truly Matters to You

Your Values or Theirs?

If you asked Jacob, he'd say he valued "adventure" and "spontaneity." He'd see people on Instagram backpacking around the world, taking risks, pivoting careers on a whim. He'd think: *Yes, that's what an interesting life looks like.*

He'd say his core values were adventure, freedom, and new experiences. It sounded good. It felt aspirational.

There was just one problem: It was completely untrue.

When he looked at how he actually spent his time and money, the truth was undeniable: He valued deep relationships, intellectual growth, and—here's the part he didn't want to admit—security and stability.

He didn't want to backpack through Southeast Asia. He wanted a dog and a home he loved coming home to.

He didn't want to pivot careers constantly. He wanted to go deep in work that mattered and get really good at it.

He didn't want constant novelty. He wanted depth, mastery, and meaningful connection with a small number of people he genuinely cared about.

The "adventurous" life he claimed to want made him miserable. He kept trying to be that person—saying yes to opportunities that drained him, feeling guilty for wanting roots and routine, judging himself as boring because he preferred depth over breadth.

The disconnect between his aspirational values (who he wished he was) and his actual values (who he actually was) created years of confusion, poor decisions, and chronic misalignment.

Everything shifted when he finally accepted the truth: Your values aren't who you want to be. They're who you are when no one's watching.

This chapter is about discovering that truth—not through aspiration, but through honest observation of how you actually live.

The Truth About Your Values

Your values aren't aspirational ideals you're trying to reach. They're already operating in your life; whether you've named them or not.

The work isn't to create new values. It's to uncover the ones already guiding you, honor them consciously, and stop betraying them for approval.

When you live from your values, everything changes:

- Decisions become clearer (you have a filter)

- Resentment decreases (you have your own back)

- Energy increases (there's no vitality leaking to misalignment)

- Relationships deepen (people see the real you)

- Success actually satisfies (because it's aligned)

You don't need to figure out who you should be. You need to honor who you already are.

Values vs. Goals: Know the Difference

Goals are destinations; specific outcomes, like lose 20 pounds or get promoted. They're binary and finite. Once reached, they're done.

Values are directions. You can never "complete" a value. If you value growth, you orient your entire life toward continuous expansion, not a one-time achievement.

Goals are checkboxes — achieve one, feel briefly satisfied, then need the next one.

Values are sustainable — when you live according to them, you experience fulfillment in the process, not just at some distant finish line.

Goals can betray values. You can get the promotion by compromising integrity, build wealth by sacrificing relationships, achieve fame by abandoning authenticity.

Clarity on your values means you can assess any goal by asking if it honors or betrays what you actually care about.

Values are the non-negotiable truths of your soul. They remain stable over time and reveal themselves not in what you *say* matters, but in how you actually spend your time, money, and energy.

They aren't aspirational — "I wish I valued health" doesn't mean you do.

They aren't virtues — honesty and kindness are universal; values are specific to you.

And they aren't roles — "being a good parent" isn't a value, but presence might be.

Soul Tax: The Cost of Value Betrayal

Before we talk about discovering your values, you need to understand what's at stake—because the cost of living out of alignment is higher than most people realize.

I call it the Soul Tax—the price you pay in energy, vitality, and aliveness when you betray what matters most to you.

Consistently acting against your core values results in what psychologists call moral injury; a condition with symptoms that overlap significantly with PTSD, including shame, guilt, depression, anxiety, and loss of meaning.[1,2]

What Values Betrayal Feels Like

Fatigue that sleep doesn't fix. You sleep 12 hours yet wake depleted because you spend your days doing things that violate your values.[3,4]

Chronic resentment. You're irritable because you're angry at yourself for abandoning your values.

Numbness. You go through the motions. You dissociate from your own life because staying present would mean feeling how out of alignment you are.

Success that feels hollow. You achieve impressive things, but they don't satisfy because they betray your values.

Physical symptoms. Tension, headaches, digestive issues. Your body knows when you're betraying yourself.

Existential emptiness. "Is this all there is?" haunts you because you're not living your actual life; you're living someone else's script.

What Values Betrayal Looks Like

Marie valued autonomy and creativity. But she took a high-paying corporate job with rigid structures. Within two years, she was on antidepressants—successful by external metrics but dying inside.

Todd valued presence and deep connection. But he built a business requiring constant travel. He achieved financial success, but his marriage was falling apart, his kids barely knew him, and he didn't have any close friends.

Jen valued integrity and authenticity. But she stayed in a relationship where she constantly censored herself. When it ended, she'd spent 5 years abandoning her values daily.

The pattern: All three were "successful," yet miserable, because external success without values alignment is just sophisticated self-abandonment.

Discover Your True Values

Now that you understand what values actually are and why they matter, let's find yours. Not the ones you wish you had; the ones already operating in your life.

The Demartini Method

Dr. John Demartini developed one of the best value identification systems I've seen. Here's a sampling of the questions[5] to get at your actual priorities:

1. What do you fill your space with most? Look at your physical environment. What dominates? Books (learning)? Photos (relationships)? Art (aesthetics)?

2. How do you spend your time? Look at your calendar. This is the most honest measure of what you value.

3. What energizes you most? What activities or topics consistently give you life force?

4. How do you spend your money? What dominates your discretionary spending?

5. Where are you most organized? What areas of your life have the highest degree of order and organization?

6. Where are you most reliable and disciplined? What do you show up for consistently without forcing yourself? That's where your values live.

7. What do you think about most? What topics occupy your mental space most consistently? Your thoughts congregate around your values.

8. What do you talk to others about most? What topics do you naturally steer conversations toward? What could you talk about endlessly?

9. What inspires you or makes you envious? When you see someone living a certain way, what about it makes you think "I want that"? The common thread reveals your values.

10. What do you love to learn about most? What topics fascinate you?

Answer all questions. Then look for themes across your answers. Your core values will appear repeatedly.

The Peak and Valley Method

Your values reveal themselves most clearly in your best and worst moments:

Peaks: Think of 3 moments when you felt most alive, fulfilled, and aligned. For each one, ask: "What was I doing?" "What values were being honored?" "What need was being met?"

Valleys: Now think of 3 moments when you felt most depleted, betrayed, or misaligned. For each one, ask: "What was I doing?" "What value was being violated?" "What boundary was being crossed?"

Your Values Hierarchy

You likely have 10-15 things you care about. But not equally.

This is your values hierarchy—some values matter more than others.

You can't honor all your values all the time. Sometimes they compete:

- Autonomy vs. Connection (freedom vs. commitment)

- Achievement vs. Presence (ambition vs. being present with loved ones)

- Security vs. Adventure (stability vs. taking risks)

- Growth vs. Comfort (stretching vs. ease)

When values conflict, you need to know which one takes precedence.

1. List your values. Based on the methods above, write down the top 10 things you value.

2. Force-rank them. Ask: "If I could only honor one value for the rest of my life, which would it be?" That becomes #1. Then ask: "If I could only honor one more, which would it be?" That becomes #2. Continue until you have your top 5.

3. Test your ranking. Look at major decisions you've made. Do they align with this hierarchy? If not, you've been betraying your values.

4. Write down your top 5 core values. These are your non-negotiables. When you betray these, you betray yourself.

Living From Your Values

Using your values as a decision-making filter in daily life is where the power lives. Audit the major domains of your life through your values lens:

- **Work/career.** Does your current role honor or violate your top values?

- **Relationships.** Do your closest relationships honor your values? Where are you tolerating value violations to keep the peace?

- **How you spend time.** What percent of your time is spent in values-aligned activities?

- **How you spend money.** Does your spending reflecting your actual values?

- **Your environment.** Does your space reflect your values?

- **Your commitments.** Which ones honor your values?

For each domain, rate your current alignment 1-10. Anything below 7 needs attention. Anything below 5 is actively harming you.

When facing any significant choice, run it through your values filter:

- Identify your top 3 relevant values and ask: "Does this option honor or violate each value?"

- Check your gut. What does your body say? Make the choice that honors your hierarchy.

When You Can't Live Your Values Right Now

Sometimes circumstances temporarily prevent you from fully honoring your values, but you can't leave the situation quite yet.

Here's what to do:

1. Acknowledge the misalignment honestly. Remind yourself: "This situation violates value of X. I'm here temporarily for Y reasons."

2. Find small ways to honor your values. Even in misaligned situations, you can create pockets of alignment.

3. Set a timeline. "I'm tolerating this misalignment for 6 months while I build my exit strategy."

The Bridge Forward

Now you know what matters to you, not what should matter or what looks impressive. What actually matters to your soul. You've identified your core values. You've done the alignment audit and seen where your life honors or betrays what you care about most.

But values without direction are just abstract principles. Knowing what matters is essential—but it's not enough.

Your values tell you what matters. Your purpose shows you where to direct that mattering.

In the next chapter, we're going to help you discover your purpose.

Let's go find it.

Chapter 7

Why You're Here

The Purpose Paradox

For years, I was obsessed with finding my purpose. Not in a healthy, curious way. In an anxious, desperate way.

I spent all my mental energy trying to reverse-engineer the perfect answer: What's the most strategic, efficient, high-impact way I can serve the most people possible? What single thing should I dedicate my life to?

My brain was constantly in overdrive, running simulations.

Should I focus on empowering women and girls? Obesity? Homelessness? Improving workplaces? I was paralyzed by the weight of finding *the* purpose—singular, definitive, impressive enough to justify my existence.

Then my very practical (and wise) mother said something that changed everything.

We were making dinner together, and I was spiraling about purpose again.

She listened patiently, then said, "Why don't you just focus on who you can help, serve, or really *see* today?"

I stared at her. "Today? That's too small. I'm trying to figure out my life purpose."

"Your life is made of days, honey." She said. "If you live each day with purpose, you'll have lived a purposeful life. You don't need to figure out the whole plan; you just need to show up for what's in front of you. Give the homeless person a dollar, hold the door for someone, or smile at a neighbor."

That one reframe unhooked me from the overwhelm. It brought me back into the present moment; out of the mental maze and into grounded clarity.

Her advice gave me a tangible path: Live *on purpose*, here and now, rather than chase some elusive capital-P purpose out on the horizon. It freed me to be creative in the moment—offering what I had to whoever crossed my path—while still working toward larger impact.

That shift taught me something powerful: You don't have to "find your purpose" before you start living *with purpose*.

The research is clear: people with purpose live seven years longer[10] and experience dramatically lower rates of Alzheimer's, stroke, and heart attacks.[11,12,13]

Purpose predicts life satisfaction more powerfully than wealth, health, or marriage.

The paradox: Most adults search for purpose, but the majority find it anxiety-inducing rather than inspiring.

Those who view purpose as something to "find" experience significantly higher existential distress than those who build it through action.

We've turned the very thing that could save us into a source of suffering by treating it as a destination instead of a daily practice.

Jungian psychoanalyst Dr. James Hollis teaches[1] that rather than asking "What do I want from life?" we should reverse the question entirely and ask:

- "What does life want from me?"

- "What wants to be expressed through me?"

This is a complete inversion of how most people approach their lives. Most of us spend decades asking: "What will make ME happy?" "What will fulfill ME?" "What can I get?"

But Hollis suggests that "something larger than your ego is trying to live itself through you." Your soul has assignments. Life itself has expectations of you.

When you stop trying to extract what you want from life and start listening for what life is asking of you, everything shifts.

You shift from anxiety about "finding" your purpose to curiosity about what wants to emerge.

You move from pressure to have it all figured out to trust that your assignment reveals itself. From ego-driven achievement to soul-aligned contribution, and from "Am I doing enough?" to "Am I listening deeply enough?"

Hollis says the question is not "What do I want from life?" but "What does the soul ask of me?"

This question aligns you with something infinitely wiser than your strategic mind; your soul.

The assignments are already there, waiting for you to get quiet enough to hear and brave enough to honor them.

What Purpose Really Is

Before we go further, let's clear up the confusion around purpose, mission, and assignments:

- **Purpose** is how you show up. It's not a thing you do. It's a way of being; the quality you bring to each moment. Yours might be to bring presence, clarity, compassion, or possibility to whatever you touch. Purpose is the *how* and *why* underneath the *what*.

- **Mission** is your throughline. It's the thread that runs through your life—the particular flavor of contribution you're here to make. For example, "helping people find their voice." Mission is more specific than purpose but less specific than a career.

- **Assignments** are the specific tasks in front of you. They're the most immediate and concrete; the specific person to serve, problem to solve, or creation to complete.

When these three align—how you show up, what you're here to contribute, and what's in front of you right now—you're living with purpose.

Purpose Leaves Breadcrumbs

Your purpose has been leaving breadcrumbs your entire life — hidden in your wounds, encoded in your gifts, written in your obsessions, and mapped in your birth chart.

You weren't missing the signs. You were simply never taught how to read them.

Your Wounds

The poet Rumi said, "The wound is the place where the light enters you." The things you've survived often point toward what you're meant to teach or facilitate for others.

Brené Brown battled shame before becoming the world's leading researcher on vulnerability.

Viktor Frankl survived concentration camps, then dedicated his life to helping others find meaning in suffering.

Tony Robbins turned a childhood marked by poverty, instability, and abuse into a lifelong mission of helping others discover what's possible for them.

Your mess becomes your message. Your trials are your training—if you let them fuel you instead of falling into victim mode.

Reflection:

- What is the hardest thing you've been through?

- What capacity did you develop to survive it?

- How could that capacity serve others?

Your Innate Talents and Gifts

Your natural gifts are abilities that emerge organically; effortless for you but difficult for others. These are things you find energizing rather than draining, and consistent across contexts.

Reflection:

- When do you lose track of time?

- What would you do unpaid?

- What energizes you?

- What do people repeatedly request from you?

- What compliments do you dismiss?

- Ask 3 people what you do better than anyone else

Your Persistent Obsessions

Your obsessions aren't random; they're your soul showing you what you're here to address.

Reflection:

- What breaks your heart? Not just sadness, what breaks you *open*?

- What can't you stop thinking about?

- What makes you irrationally angry? This reveals what you value.

- What would you work on unpaid?

Your Ikigai: The Convergence Point

Ikigai is a Japanese concept meaning "reason for being"—the convergence of 4 elements: what you love, what you're good at, what the world needs, and what people will pay for.[3,4]

Map your Ikigai: Draw four overlapping circles:

Circle 1 - What you love:

- What you're extremely passionate about

- Activities where you lose track of time

- Topics you are endlessly fascinated by

Circle 2 - What you're good at:

- Natural talents and developed skills

- What others seek you out for

Circle 3 - What the world needs:

- What problems need solving?

- What breaks your heart?

- What injustice needs fighting?

Circle 4 - What you can be paid for:

- What skills do people already pay for?

- What problems would people pay to solve?

Look for overlaps. Where do they intersect? That's your Ikigai.

Your Astrological Blueprint

Whether you view astrology as cosmic truth or psychological archetype, it's a powerful self-reflection tool. I'm referring to astronomy-based birth chart analysis; not magazine horoscopes. Kings, queens, and empire-builders consulted this system for millennia. Your birth chart maps your innate wiring and core life themes, including purpose markers.[8]

How to get started:

1. Generate your birth chart. You'll need your birth date, exact birth time, and birth location. Generate your free chart at www.astro.com.

2. Explore your purpose indicators. Dig into the placements that reveal your calling. You can use AI to explore what each placement means.

Key placements:

- Rising sign (Ascendant): The energy you're here to express

- North Node: Your soul's evolutionary direction

- Midheaven (MC): Your public calling and contribution

- Saturn placement: Where your most important work lies

3. Work with someone. A skilled astrologer can synthesize patterns you'd never see alone. I recommend Debra Silverman, astrologer to Sting, Madonna, and others. Find her at: www.debrasilvermanastrology.com.

From Finding Purpose To Living It

You don't need perfect clarity to start living purposefully. Perfect clarity is often just an excuse to delay.

Stop asking: "What's my purpose?" and start asking: "Who can I serve today? What assignment is in front of me?"

You don't discover purpose in your head. It emerges through engaged action.[9] Instead of waiting for your perfect purpose, live it:

- Show up for what's in front of you: The person who needs help today. The small act of kindness no one else notices.

- Bring your gifts: Whatever the task, bring your natural capacities. If your gift is presence, bring that to the mundane meeting. If it's clarity, bring that to the confused conversation.

- Honor your values: In each choice, ask: "Does this align with what matters most to me?"

- Serve what needs serving: Not what's most impressive or visible. What actually needs tending to right now?

- Trust emergence: Purpose won't arrive as a lightning bolt. It will emerge from small, consistent acts of showing up fully where you are.

Your purpose isn't something to find. It's something you become through aligned action.

The Seasons of Purpose

Purpose isn't static. What's true for you at 25 might not be at 45. The assignment that called to you in your 30s might be completed in your 40s, and a new one emerges.

Common Seasons

Your 20s: Learning and capacity building. Primary assignment: Develop skills, explore possibilities. This season is about breadth and experiences.

Your 30s: Building and establishing. Primary assignment: Go deep, commit, build something meaningful. This season is about depth.

Your 40s: Mastery and contribution. Primary assignment: Leverage your expertise, teach what you've learned. This season is about impact.

Your 50s: Integration and wisdom sharing. Primary assignment: Integrate all experiences into wisdom. This season is about synthesis and transmission.

Your 60s+: Legacy and essence. Primary assignment: Distill your life into its essential contributions. This season is about essence.

Signs your assignment is shifting:

- What used to fulfill you now feels empty

- New problems are capturing your attention

- Old goals have lost their emotional charge

- You feel restless even though things are going well

The Bridge Forward

You came into this chapter perhaps hoping to finally answer the question that's been following you: "What am I here for?"

And maybe you've realized that the question itself was the problem — not because it's wrong to ask, but because it assumes purpose is something hidden, something you have to dig up before your real life can begin.

It isn't. Purpose is already here, woven into your wounds, your gifts, your obsessions, and the assignments life keeps placing in front of you.

It doesn't require a grand revelation. It requires attention. It requires you to stop performing a life that looks impressive and start living one that feels true.

So begin where you are. Serve who's in front of you. Bring what only you can bring.

And trust that a life lived with daily intention will, over time, reveal a purpose far bigger than anything your strategic mind could have engineered.

The breadcrumbs are already there.

Follow them...

Chapter 8

Feeding Your Soul in a World That Starves It

The Priceless $400 Therapy Session

"I don't know why I'm here," Tim said, staring at his hands.

"I'm not depressed. Nothing's actually wrong."

His therapist waited.

"Objectively, my life is great. Good job. Solid marriage. Healthy kids. But I wake up every morning, and it's like...I'm watching my own life through plexiglass. Everything feels muted."

Dr. Chen leaned forward. "Tim, when was the last time you felt truly alive? Not productive. Not anxious....viscerally alive present in your experience?"

The question landed like a stone in still water. Thud.

Tim's mind scrolled backward. Days. Weeks. Months. His throat tightened.

"You're not broken," she said quietly. "You're starving. And you've been trying to satisfy a soul hunger with ego food."

Tim left furious. *Soul hunger? What kind of woo-woo bullshit was that?*

But the question followed him home. Slept next to him that night. *When was the last time you felt truly alive?*

A week later, at 6:47 AM on a Tuesday, everything changed.

Tim stood at the kitchen counter, waiting for the Keurig.

November light set the neighbor's maple ablaze. His daughter's finger painting caught his eye: Magenta trees, an emerald sun, and three people holding hands. The scent of hazelnut filled the air. Tim paused as a crimson cardinal landed on the fence.

And something in his chest...opened.

For the first time in years, he wasn't anywhere but right *here*.

The feeling rose slowly, like water finding its level. Something deeper than happiness...something that caught in his throat.

"Thank you," he whispered to no one.

The tears came fast.

42 years old, crying over coffee, a bird, and a kid's drawing. Because he suddenly understood: He'd been so busy optimizing his life that he'd stopped experiencing it.

That Thursday, he went back to therapy. "I felt it," Tim said. "I felt alive. Just making coffee. But for two minutes, I was actually there. It's like I'd been living in black and white and suddenly everything was in Technicolor."

Dr. Chen leaned back. "So the question isn't what's wrong with you anymore. Now you know what you're hungry for."

Tim nodded. "It's not more success. Not a bigger house. It's...*that*...what I felt in those two minutes of actually being alive in my own life."

Your Story

You're not depressed. You're not broken. You're starving — and you've been feeding the wrong hunger.

You've spent your life chasing what society promised would complete you. The title. The income. The relationship. The body. The recognition. And somewhere along the way, you achieved some of it — maybe all of it.

So why do you still feel empty?

Because what doesn't feed your soul will always leave you hungry.

You can eat forever without feeling full if what you're eating doesn't satisfy you.

Tim learned this standing in his kitchen at 6:47 a.m., as the steam rose from his coffee. No agenda. No device. No performance. Just a man, a quiet morning, and the rare experience of being fully present in his own life. Two minutes of being fully alive taught him more than two decades of achievement ever had.

So now you've done the work. You've determined what matters most to you. You've discovered your unique assignments and reasons for being here. You've begun to understand who you actually are beneath the roles.

But if you're like most people, you're still not sure what your soul needs — or how to satisfy it. The self-awareness arrived, but the emptiness didn't leave.

This is where most people get stuck. They do the inner work, gain self-awareness, and then wonder: "I know myself better now — so why do I still feel like shit?"

The answer is brutal in its simplicity: Knowing yourself and nourishing yourself are two entirely different skills. You've been developing the first. What you need now is the second.

Most people never learn it — because no one ever told them it existed.

Needs: Invisible Engines

In his work, psychologist Abraham Maslow distinguished deficiency needs from being needs.[1,2]

Most people spend their entire lives trapped in the first category, wondering why they never feel satisfied.

Beneath every desire, behavior, and choice lies a need you're trying to meet, whether you're aware of it or not.

When you don't understand what you truly need, you chase substitutes that can never satisfy.

It's like being desperately thirsty and trying to quench it with saltwater. You keep drinking, keep consuming, keep seeking—and the thirst only grows.

Deficiency Needs: The Survival Trap

Deficiency needs drive you when they're absent, creating gnawing anxiety that won't quit until they're met.

These include physiological needs (food, rest, shelter), safety (financial security, stability), love, acceptance, and esteem (respect, validation, recognition).

When these needs go unmet, your motivation becomes a survival strategy. You hustle for worth, perform for approval, and post for likes to feel secure.

You're operating from deficiency—trying to fill what's lacking rather than express what's possible.

And this is where you're easiest to manipulate.

Advertising and social media exploit these deficiency needs with surgical precision, keeping you perpetually wanting but never satisfied. Because your satisfaction isn't their goal; your insatiable hunger is.

A satisfied person stops consuming and focuses on creating. An anxious, insecure, unsatisfied person keeps buying, scrolling, seeking.

Junk Food Substitutes For Soul Food

What you chase often stems from soul hungers disguised as material desires: junk food substitutes for real nourishment:

- **Authentic connection** is replaced by likes and followers.

- **Creative expression** becomes passive consumption.

- **Feeling alive** is numbed by endless scrolling.

- **Meaningful work** is replaced with impressive credentials.

Dig under what you think you want to reveal what you actually need:

- **You want wealth** because you need freedom and autonomy.

- **You want the titles** because you need to feel valuable.

- **You want to look perfect** because you need to feel worthy.

The want is the surface desire, but the need is what you're actually after.

Being Needs: The Soul's Three Hungers

After working with thousands of people and synthesizing decades of research, I've seen a pattern emerge: all our surface wants and endless pursuits stem from three fundamental soul hungers:

1. Becoming is the need to feel alive in your own experience, express your authentic nature, and grow into your full potential.

2. Belonging is the need to connect deeply, contribute to others, and feel like you matter.

3. Beyond is the need to transcend the small self and touch the infinite.

These aren't nice-to-haves. They're essential requirements for human flourishing.

When they go unmet, you don't just feel neutral; you feel hollow, lost, wondering what it's all for.

You achieve impressive things and feel nothing. You acquire what you thought would make you happy and still feel empty.

Because you've been feeding deficiency needs while your soul starves.

The shift from deficiency-based to soul-based living is the shift from survival to flourishing. From chasing success to prove your worth, to expressing your gifts because they're meant to be shared. From working out of anxiety and scarcity, to creating from abundance and alignment.

Your soul doesn't need what society is selling.

It needs what it's always needed: To become who you're meant to be, to matter to others, and to be part of something greater than yourself.

Feed these hungers, and everything else falls into place.

NEED 1: BECOMING

What It Is and Why It Matters

Becoming is your soul's hunger to feel alive, express its authentic nature, and expand into its full potential.

It's those moments when existence shifts from monochrome to Technicolor—when you're so engaged that time dissolves, so enthralled you can barely catch your breath, so expansive you feel superhuman, and you catch yourself thinking: *This is what I was made for.*

This isn't about self-improvement in the hustle-culture sense. It's about unfolding—like an acorn becoming an oak tree[3]. It simply becomes what it already is.

You were not born to stay small, safe, or static. Something in you knows this.

When your need for becoming is met, you experience deep vitality, purpose, and authentic satisfaction.

You feel like yourself—not performing a role, but expressing your true nature freely and fully.

The alternative is a slow death of the spirit.

Palliative care nurse Bronnie Ware spent years sitting with people in the final weeks of their lives. In her book *The Top Five Regrets of the Dying*, she revealed that the most common deathbed regret isn't about mistakes made — it's about the life unlived, the self unexpressed, the potential quietly abandoned somewhere along the way.[4]

The Three Dimensions of Becoming

1. Aliveness is the presence to show up fully to your experience, engaging all your senses, and seeing the extraordinary in the mundane.

2. Expression is the bridge between your inner world and outer reality: The courage to share your authentic voice, creative impulses, and unique gifts.

3. Growth is the expansion; the willingness to stretch beyond your comfort zone, develop new capacities, and evolve into the fullest version of yourself.

Self-Assessment

Aliveness Check:

- When was the last time you felt fully present and engaged—so absorbed that you lost track of time?

- Are you moving through your days on autopilot, or are you genuinely awake to your experience?

Expression Check:

- What parts of yourself are you suppressing?

- Are you living *your* life, or performing for approval?

Growth Check:

- Where are you stuck, stagnant, or playing it safe when your soul wants to grow?

- Are you becoming wiser, stronger, and more capable, or are you the same person you were a year ago?

Meet the Need For Becoming - Aliveness

Aliveness is feeling fully present and engaged with your existence—awake to the full spectrum of being human, not numbed out or on autopilot.

Ordinary moments become extraordinary. Colors become more vivid. Conversations deepen. Time slows down. You remember what it feels like to be truly *here*.

Three Essential Practices To Get Started

1. Create Digital Boundaries

Your smartphone is an attention-extraction device pulling you out of the present moment. Ban phones at dinner and the bedroom, and keep them pocketed while waiting in line.

Notice what emerges when you stop reflexively reaching for distraction. Conversations deepen, observations sharpen, life becomes more vivid.

2. Savor

Engage all your senses to extract maximum richness from each moment.

Notice the fabric texture against your skin. Listen to a song's intricate melody. Inhale the layered aroma of your coffee. Small choices like these accumulate into feeling fully alive.

3. Cultivate Gratitude

Gratitude trains your brain to notice what's going well instead of fixating on what's missing.

When my neighbor's teenage son took his own life, the weight of grief was crushing. He and his wife began a ritual: Over dinner, they'd each share one "great bit" from their day—however small—as an anchor back to living.

At first, finding anything felt impossible. But gradually, he caught himself scanning his day for small moments—a favorite song on the radio, a stunning sunset, a child's smile, a friend's joke. He wasn't just noticing these moments, he was actively seeking them out, looking for grace in the ordinary hours.

Months later, he told me, "I'm still grieving—I'll always be grieving—but I'm not *only* grieving anymore."

Gratitude doesn't erase pain. It expands your capacity to hold both grief and beauty, pain and small mercies, brokenness and reverence for life.

Meet the Need for Becoming - Expression

When you honor your soul's need for expression, you feel expansive, authentic, aligned. When you silence it, you disappear behind a mask—present but not really there.

Expression is the bridge between who you are inside and how you show up in the world. It's the practice of making your inner truth visible.

Three Essential Practices To Get Started

1. Stop Self-Suppressing

We silence ourselves in a thousand subtle ways—swallowing our truth to keep the peace, numbing feelings, performing positivity when we're breaking inside, shrinking ourselves to fit spaces never meant for us.

But what we suppress doesn't disappear. It waits, accumulates, and eventually erupts as rage, illness, collapse.

When I lost my father years ago, I buried myself in work. Grief was inconvenient. And I worried that if I let myself feel it, I would never recover. So I pushed it down, muscled through, and performed strength.

The cost? Bone-deep exhaustion. A constant sense of running from something I couldn't name, always on edge, always ready to detonate.

Until one evening, completely alone in my living room, something inside me finally broke open. I collapsed on the floor and sobbed for hours—the kind where you can't catch your breath, where your whole body heaves because the dam has finally burst.

That ugly cry taught me we cannot heal from what we refuse to feel.

This past year, when my baby brother and grandmother passed within two days of each other, I approached the grief differently.

Instead of pushing down the pain, I allowed the emotions to come, moving through me like waves—sometimes overwhelming, sometimes gentle.

But because I let them flow instead of fighting them, they never took me down completely. And in that allowing, I've found healing.

2. Notice What's Trying to Be Expressed Through You

Your soul speaks through your passions, inexplicable interests, natural talents, and persistent dreams.

These aren't random; they're breadcrumbs leading toward your unique expression.

The form doesn't matter; what matters is that it's genuinely yours. What excites you? What can't you stop talking about? That's your soul trying to express itself through you.

3. Treat Creativity As a Responsibility

Author Julia Cameron said, "Creativity is God's gift to us. Using our creativity is our gift back to God." This reframes creative expression not as a luxury or hobby, but as a sacred responsibility.[5]

For you, authentic creation might mean expressing emotions through music, building something, cooking a new recipe, nurturing relationships, solving complex problems, or creative parenting.

The specific medium matters less than your complete engagement with it.

Meet the Need for Becoming: Growth

Within each of us lies a reservoir of unique skills, talents, and experiences waiting to be unleashed.

When you speak with genuinely fulfilled people, their joy doesn't stem from titles or possessions; it comes from personal transformation, from who they become as they actualize their potential.

Three Essential Practices To Get Started

1. Live With Arete

The ancient Greeks had a word for living at your highest potential: Arete. Not perfection; that's impossible and soul-crushing to chase. But excellence. The full expression of your capabilities.

Aristotle understood that human flourishing requires this ongoing pursuit. Not for external validation, but because stagnation is a form of dying.

At 95, Warren Buffett, one of the wealthiest people in the world, still spends 80% of his day reading, not because he needs to keep up, but because he's genuinely curious about how the world works.

Living with Arete means treating your life as a craft you're constantly refining. Become insatiably curious—reading across disciplines, finding new podcasts, learning a new skill, taking courses on something that fascinates you.

2. Treat Challenges As Curriculum

Challenges aren't obstacles to growth; they *are* the growth. Every difficulty you face is an assignment designed to develop a capacity you don't yet have.

Every night at dinner, Sara Blakely's father asked the same question: "What did you fail at today?" Blakely, who went on to build Spanx into a billion-dollar company, credits that ritual with giving her the ability to see failure not as a verdict, but as a path.[6]

Volunteer for the stretch assignment everyone avoids at work. Have the difficult conversation instead of letting resentment build. Attempt something you might fail at publicly. Build the muscle of transcending discomfort.

3. Seek Feedback Like Your Life Depends On It

Blind spots are called that because you can't see them. You need others to show you what you can't see about yourself.

Ray Dalio built Bridgewater into one of the world's most successful hedge funds by creating a "culture of radical truth and transparency." Everyone, regardless of rank, is expected to give and receive brutally honest feedback.[7]

It's uncomfortable. But it's how you get better. Find people who care enough about you to tell you the truth and thank them for the hard truths they share.

NEED 2: BELONGING

What It Is and Why It Matters

Belonging is your soul's hunger for genuine connection, meaningful contribution, and feeling significant. It's the need to be truly seen, known, and valued.

The longest-running study on human happiness found the quality of your relationships is the single most significant predictor of your well-being and happiness.[8]

But modern culture mistakes contact for connection. You can have thousands of friends online and still be profoundly lonely. The loneliness epidemic[9] isn't about being alone; it's about being disconnected.

The Three Dimensions of Belonging

1. Connection is being in relationships where you can be fully yourself and still belong; not performing, but being known for who you actually are.

2. Contribution is being of service and leaving the world better than you found it. It's the impact you make on others.

3. Significance is feeling that your life has meaning and value, both to yourself and to others. It's recognizing you hold a unique place in the human story no one else can fill.

Self-Assessment

Connection Check:

- Who truly sees and knows me, not just the version I perform for them?

- In how many of my relationships can I be fully myself without editing?

Contribution Check:

- Where am I contributing to the lives of others?

- What gifts or skills do I have that I'm not fully sharing with the world?

Significance Check:

- Do I feel like my life matters; to myself and to others?

- Am I building something or just consuming and surviving?

Meet The Need For Belonging - Connection

We're hyperconnected yet profoundly isolated.

We've mistaken contact for connection. We have thousands of online connections and no one to call at 2 a.m. We have audiences, but no intimates.

The difference is whether you feel truly seen, understood, and valued — not your highlight reel, not the version of you that performs well in public. You. The unedited one.

Three Essential Practices To Get Started

1. Find Your People

When the soul lacks authentic connection, we experience a particular kind of suffering that transcends ordinary loneliness. We feel unmoored, hollow, perpetually restless; as if something essential is missing.

Reflection:

- Who in my life elevates and expands me?

- Who drains me or keeps me stuck in old patterns?

- Who do I feel like my best self around?

This isn't elitism; it's basic self-respect.

Your energy is finite. Your time is limited. You deserve to spend it with people who truly see you, who honor you, and make you more yourself , not less.

2. Embrace Vulnerability As Currency

Our culture frames vulnerability as weakness, but in relationships, it functions as powerful connection currency.

When you share something real—a struggle, a fear, a dream—you create space for others to do the same. This transforms strangers into friends and friends into soul companions.

Some think asking for help makes them look weak or burdens others. The opposite is true. Asking for help tells the other person "I trust you. I see you as capable and value your wisdom."

And research shows that when people help you, they experience a "helper's high"; a release of oxytocin, dopamine, serotonin, and endorphins.[17,18]

3. Go Deeper In Conversation

Moving beyond small talk requires curiosity, courage, and genuine listening.

Human connection scientist Vanessa Van Edwards suggests a three-level progression.[12]

See if you can get beyond the surface:

- Surface: Daily highlights and current projects

- Meaningful: Goals and what's weighing on someone's heart

- Deep: How people feel misunderstood, what shaped their personality, and their proudest moments

Meet the Need for Belonging - Contribution

From Aristotle to modern researchers like Adam Grant, the answer has been consistent: Human flourishing requires purpose beyond the self.

We need to feel useful—to leave the world better than we found it and serve others.

When this need goes unmet, we lose our sense of meaning, and belonging.

Three Essential Practices To Get Started

1. Shift From Getting to Giving

When you shift from "What do I get?" to "What can I give?" everything changes.

Contribution is active engagement with the world beyond yourself. Anxiety quiets. Emptiness recedes. The victim narrative loses its grip because you're no longer the passive recipient of life; you're an active part of it.[10] And paying it forward has a whole cascade of positive effects, including levels of happiness and physical health.[23, 24]

Ask yourself weekly:

- What three people could I uplift this week? Perhaps it's a kind message, a helpful resource, a surprise coffee, a few minutes of full presence.

- What are three gifts I have that I haven't fully shared lately (skills, insights, hard-earned wisdom, a resource)? Choose one and offer it.

2. Co-Elevate

Management thinker Keith Ferrazzi calls it "co-elevation."[11] Matthew McConaughey describes it as "do for the I, that is for the We." This is about creating win-win dynamics and mutually beneficial solutions.

Life isn't zero-sum. The choice between selfishness OR selflessness is survival mode thinking. We're operating in a different paradigm; one where your flourishing and others' flourishing are complimentary, not competing interests.

One of the most sustainable and fulfilling ways to live is co-elevating, which is finding the win-win, or even win-win-win in every situation.

Ways to do it:

- **The "and" question.** Replace "either/or" thinking with "and" thinking. Instead of "Should I prioritize my needs or theirs?" ask "How can I honor my needs *and* serve theirs?"

- **The generous ask.** When making an ask, do it in a way that benefits both parties. Instead of "Can you help me with this project?" try "I'm working on X—would you be interested in collaborating? I think it could showcase your skills too." This transforms requests into opportunities for mutual elevation.

- **Celebrate others' wins as your own.** When someone succeeds, genuinely celebrate as if it were your own victory. Their rising expands what's possible for everyone. This dissolves scarcity thinking and reinforces an abundance mindset.

3. Live on Purpose

Contribution can be philanthropy or volunteering, but it lives in the small moments too: Holding the door for someone, genuinely connecting with your barista instead of staring at your phone, or offering help to a neighbor.

These moments are not insignificant. They are, in many ways, the point. A single genuine interaction can shift someone's entire day — and your own.

It doesn't take much to create ripples of impact, just intention.

Meet the Need for Belonging - Significance

In a world where acts of violence and deaths of despair dominate headlines, we often blame ideology, politics, or mental health.

Beneath many of these tragedies lies the same unmet need: The longing to matter.

When people feel invisible or unneeded, the psyche contorts into dangerous shapes. In this era of unprecedented disconnection, an astonishing number of people are drowning in feeling empty and insignificant.

Significance is feeling your life has meaning and value; that you hold a unique place in the larger human story.

The need for significance isn't vanity. It's wired into us.

Beneath nearly every human behavior lives the same fundamental question: Do I matter?

Three Essential Practices To Get Started

1. Meet It Consciously

The antidote isn't transcending the need for significance, it's meeting it consciously through:

- **Authentic expression of your gifts.** There's a reason your unique combination of talents, perspectives, and experiences exist. In expressing what's genuinely yours, you create value that only you can create.

- **Relationships where you're genuinely valued.** Being someone's trusted confidant, go-to person in crisis, or the one who remembers their birthday carries profound significance.

- **Work that contributes something meaningful.** Whether you're solving problems that improve people's lives, creating beauty that uplifts spirits, or serving needs that would otherwise go unmet, your labor serves something beyond yourself.

You don't need to be significant to everyone. You need to know that your life means something to someone, most importantly, yourself.

2. Become Irreplaceable to a Small Circle

Instead of trying to be known by thousands, become indispensable to a few.

Be the friend who shows up during hard times, the colleague who invests in others, or the neighbor who notices when someone's struggling.

3. Track Your Positive Impact

Keep a "Significance Journal", tracking the moments when you made a difference. Over time, it becomes concrete, undeniable evidence that your life creates ripples. On the hard days, when doubt is loudest, read it. It has a way of cutting through the noise.

NEED 3: BEYOND

Note: I use God, Universe, and the Divine interchangeably here. Whether you resonate with religious language, scientific concepts, or spiritual terms, they all point toward the same reality: Something vast, intelligent, and larger than any single life. Take the language that fits and leave the rest.

What It Is and Why It Matters

Beyond is your soul's need to touch something infinite; to experience something vast and sacred beyond individual existence. Your soul knows it's part of something larger and hungers for experiences that remind you of this.

When life becomes only about ego concerns, a certain emptiness sets in that no achievement can fill.

This isn't about religious belief, but rather, the human capacity for experiences that crack your heart open and reconnect you to the mystery of existence.

Research shows, people who regularly connect to something larger than themselves have significantly lower rates of depression and anxiety,[19] greater resilience, enhanced creativity, and deeper purpose.[20,21]

The Three Dimensions of Beyond

1. Peak Experiences are moments when time stops, ego dissolves, and you're overwhelmed by beauty, vastness, or mystery that feels truer than ordinary life.

2. Spiritual Connection is direct personal experience of the sacred; not religious doctrine, but the felt sense of being connected to a presence that transcends your self.

3. Transcendence is the dissolution of ego and the experience of unity and interconnection with all existence.

Self-Assessment

Peak Experiences Check:

- When was the last time I felt genuine awe, stopped in my tracks by beauty or vastness?

- Can I still be moved to tears by beauty or wonder?

Spiritual Connection Check:

- Do I have a practice that connects me to something larger than myself?

- Am I living from cynicism or openness to mystery?

Transcendence Check:

- Do I feel the boundary between me and others dissolve?

- Do I forget myself entirely in service, creation, or presence?

Meet the Need For Beyond - Peak Experiences

The word "transcendence" derives from the Latin *trans*, meaning "beyond," and *scandere*, "to climb."

It means rising above the limited perspective of ego-consciousness to touch something sacred and timeless.

Psychologist Abraham Maslow termed these moments "peak experiences", or spontaneous glimpses of transcendence that can arise in everyday life.

Three Essential Practices To Get Started

1. Cultivate Awe

Why do we stop to stare at a stunning sunset? Why does a piece of music move us to tears? Or witnessing a stranger's kindness crack our hearts open?

Because awe pauses the ego and lets the soul breathe.

Research shows that experiencing awe doesn't just feel good, it transforms us.

It expands our perception of time, dissolves stress and impatience, and shifts our focus away from self-centered preoccupations.[13]

Awe isn't reserved for extraordinary experiences.

It's available in everyday moments such as a child's uninhibited laughter, golden-hour light filtering through the window, the moment a song gives you chills, an elderly couple holding hands on a park bench.

How to do it:

- **Slow down enough to notice.** Awe can't penetrate a mind moving at 100 mph.

- **Seek vastness.** Look at the night sky, stand at the edge of the ocean, witness anything that dwarfs you in the best way.

- **Pay attention to beauty.** Art, music, architecture, nature—whatever stops you in your tracks.

2. Immerse Yourself in Nature

Time in nature is like a reset button for overstimulated nervous systems. It pulls us out of mental noise and reconnects us with something deeply nourishing.

Nature teaches what civilization has made us forget: That we are part of a vast, perfect, interconnected ecosystem.

The key: Stop waiting for the perfect nature experience. Nature doesn't have to mean wilderness. A single tree, a patch of sky, your hands in soil—these count.

How to do it:

- **Weave nature into your existing routine.** Take your morning coffee outside, eat lunch in a park, or take phone calls while on a walk.

- **Bring nature inside.** get a few plants, open windows to hear birds, or work near a window.

- **Commit to five minutes outside daily.** Step outside barefoot, sit on your stoop at sunrise, or stand under a tree during lunch.

3. Create Space For Deep Presence

Peak experiences often emerge not from doing more, but from being more fully present to what's already here.[14]

The moments of deep presence—watching your child sleep, holding a loved one, sitting with someone in their grief—where you're so completely here that everything else falls away. This is where you touch the eternal in the ordinary.

Practice sacred pauses throughout your day:

- Before eating, stop and truly see your food.

- Before entering your home, pause at the threshold and arrive fully.

- Before speaking to someone you love, take a breath and choose to be completely present.

Meet the Need for Beyond - Spiritual Connection

While the terms are often confused, spirituality and religion are not the same, and they serve different functions in the human quest.

Religion tends to be about the external: The doctrine, the ritual, the institution. At its best, it offers something genuinely valuable — community, continuity, a shared moral framework, and structured pathways toward the divine. At its worst, it subordinates and divides.

But it cannot guarantee the experience of the sacred. That is spirituality's domain.

Spirituality is available to everyone. It requires no membership, no intermediary, and no permission.

It is not something you inherit, join, or perform — it is something you encounter, usually in the quiet places that organized religion cannot reach.

Where religion can be handed down, spirituality must be discovered. It cannot be institutionalized or outsourced, because no external authority can tell you what you encountered in your own interior, or whether it was real.

Three Essential Practices To Get Started

1. Reclaim Direct Connection

Throughout most of human history, prior to organized religion, direct personal connection with the divine was natural and accessible to all; no church intermediaries required.[16]

The Gnostic tradition exemplifies this approach, viewing the divine as an inner presence within everyone. This perfectly aligns with Jesus's teaching: "The kingdom of heaven is within you."

The divine is already inside us. Our only work is removing the barriers that prevent us from experiencing what's always been there.[22]

How to do it:

Create an ongoing conversation with the divine. Whether through traditional prayers or throughout your day, regular dialogue deepens your spiritual connection.

2. Establish a Daily Spiritual Practice

Consistency matters more than intensity. Even 5 minutes a day builds the connection more effectively than occasional sessions.

Choose a practice that resonates with your soul. Personally, I like the silent pause and gratitude walk.

- **The silent pause.** Sit in silence and observe your breath, your thoughts, the space between them. Sometimes the most powerful practice is simply being: no technique, no agenda, just stillness and allowing whatever wants to emerge.

- **The gratitude walk.** If you find it difficult to sit still, take your practice on the move. I combine my morning walk with a gratitude practice—expressing thanks for all I've been given and what's yet to come. It's simple, profound, and it sets the tone for everything that follows.

3. Notice Synchronicities

Pay attention to meaningful coincidences, perfect timing, and unexpected helpers. That person who appeared exactly when you needed them. The book that fell off the shelf with the exact answer you were seeking. The intuition that saved you. The delay that protected you from disaster.

These aren't accidents. They're breadcrumbs pointing toward the larger intelligence guiding your life. When you start recognizing synchronicity, you begin to trust that you're being held, guided, and loved by something far wiser than your anxious ego mind.

Carl Jung understood this profoundly in saying synchronicity is how the universe communicates with those paying attention. Your soul is always in conversation with the cosmos.[15]

Practice: For the next week, keep a synchronicity log. Each evening, write down one moment that felt like more than coincidence — an unexpected connection, a perfectly timed encounter, a solution that arrived without being forced. Don't analyze it. Just record it. Most people notice that the synchronicities were always happening — and they simply weren't paying attention.

Meet The Need For Beyond - Transcendence

At the deepest level, the soul yearns for union with the infinite; that boundless creative force that some call God, others name Source, Universe, or Divine Consciousness.

This longing transcends the physical realm and speaks to a hunger for something eternal, sacred, and numinous.

Three Essential Practices To Get Started

1. Cultivate Stillness

In our culture of constant doing, simply *being* becomes a radical act. Sit, breathe, and listen. The divine speaks in whispers, not shouts.

Transcendence isn't something you achieve through effort; it's what emerges when you stop trying to achieve anything. When the mental commentary quiets. When the grasping ceases. When you simply *are*.

Create daily moments of complete stillness. No inputs, no mantras, no techniques. Just being present to what is.

In that spacious silence, the boundaries of self begin to soften. The illusion of separation becomes transparent. You remember what you've always been.

2. Practice Contemplation in Daily Life

Transcendence is accessible in ordinary moments when you're fully present.

Washing dishes becomes meditation when you're completely present to warm water, light on glass, the act of cleaning. Walking becomes prayer when you feel each footfall, witness each breath. Eating becomes communion when you're fully present to taste, texture, scent—the universe feeding itself through you.

The practice is to be fully *here*. Don't multitask. Don't rush. Don't escape into thought. In complete presence, the separate self dissolves, and transcendence emerges.

3. Recognize You've Never Been Separate

The truth is, there's nothing to achieve because you've never been separate.

You are not a drop trying to merge with the ocean. You are the ocean, experiencing itself as a drop.

The boundary was always illusory. The separation was conceptual, never actual.

Every spiritual practice, every glimpse beyond the ego simply removes the veils that obscure this truth: You are the infinite expressing itself as this particular form.

Integration

The soul needs for Becoming, Belonging, and Beyond aren't separate pursuits. They're interconnected pathways that amplify each other, creating an upward spiral of flourishing.

You don't need to work on all three simultaneously. Start where the hunger is strongest:

- Feeling numb or sleepwalking through your life? Begin with Becoming—Aliveness

- Feeling isolated or performative? Begin with Belonging—Connection

- Feeling spiritually empty? Begin with Beyond—Peak Experiences

What's Next

You've done the deep work of Part 2.

You know how you lost yourself. You've found what was there before the loss. You've clarified your values, identified your contribution, and learned what it actually takes to feed your soul.

This is profound work. Most people never do it. They live their entire lives running someone else's programming, performing someone else's values, pursuing someone else's definition of purpose, and starving their soul.

But you're different now. You've turned inward. You've done the excavation. You've remembered who you actually are and what makes life worth living.

Now comes the hardest part: Taking all of this internal clarity and translating it into your actual life.

Because you can know yourself deeply, clarify your values completely, identify your purpose clearly—and still be living a life that violates all of it. Insight without action is just sophisticated procrastination.

In Part 3, we're going to take everything you've discovered about yourself and help you build a life from that foundation.

We're going to help you make the hard decisions, have the difficult conversations, set the necessary boundaries, and take the courageous actions required to close the gap between who you truly are and how you're currently living.

The discovery phase is complete.

Now it's time to build.

PART 3 - A Life That's Actually Yours

Chapter 9

Build Your Foundation

Fill Your Cup First

Victoria stared at her phone for 20 minutes, composing a simple text to decline a lunch invitation.

Her fingers hovered over the keyboard. Delete. Retype Delete again.

The truth was simpler and harder.

She was exhausted. Bone-deep, can't-think-straight, running-on-fumes exhausted. And this lunch with someone who would talk past her for two hours while she smiled and nodded, would drain what little she had left.

But saying that felt...mean. Selfish. Like she was being dramatic.

Her hand moved toward the usual response: "Sounds great! See you then!"

But something stopped her. Not dramatically...just quietly.

She deleted it. Took a breath. And typed something she'd never said before: "I need to rest today. Let's do it another time." Her finger hesitated over send. Then she pressed it.

You can't flourish from an empty cup. You can't give from depletion. You can't sustain transformation when your foundation is crumbling.

Self-care isn't selfish; it's the strategic prerequisite for everything else.

All the inner work in the world won't save you if your body is crashing, your nervous system is fried, and you're mentally drained.

Flourishing requires more than internal work. It demands practical foundations—the daily structures that protect your energy, honor your needs, and keep you aligned when life gets chaotic.

Your body is the vehicle through which you experience life. When that vehicle is breaking down, running on empty, or stuck in survival mode, everything else suffers.

You can't think clearly when sleep-deprived, regulate emotions when your blood sugar crashes, access flow states when chronically inflamed, or feel inspired when exhausted.

This chapter is about optimizing your vitality and energy so you can live in alignment and be the best version of yourself.

Let's start with the foundation: Your physical body.

Sleep: The Non-Negotiable

There's a reason professional athletes prioritize sleep as much as training.

Sleep isn't a luxury; it's a biological necessity you ignore at your peril.

Just one night of sleep deprivation reduces prefrontal cortex activity by 18%.[1] That's the part of your brain responsible for emotional regulation, and impulse control.

Exhausted people either blow up at others or become people-pleasers because they lack the cognitive resources to resist social pressure. You become a worse version of yourself—reactive, impulsive, unable to hold boundaries.

In addition to preventing obesity, and other causes of mortality,[3] sleep cleans your brain.

The glymphatic system[2], the brain's waste removal mechanism, flushes out harmful proteins linked to various diseases.

How to Optimize Sleep:

- Maintain a consistent sleep schedule, even on weekends

- Create a cool (65-68°F), dark, and quiet environment

- Avoid blue light before bed and caffeine late

- Develop a wind-down ritual that signals rest mode

Prioritize sleep like your life depends on it. Because it does.

Nutrient Density: Food as Medicine

Chronic inflammation is linked to virtually every chronic disease: heart disease, cancer, diabetes, Alzheimer's, autoimmune conditions, and depression. It keeps your nervous system in threat mode.[4]

When your body is inflamed, everything feels more dangerous. Your threshold for stress drops. You overreact to minor inconveniences. You can't access higher thinking. Your body becomes your enemy instead of your ally.[6]

Personally, I've migrated toward a cleaner, more plant-based diet over the years. But regardless of which diet protocol you follow, the real win is nutrient density—extracting maximum micronutrients from every calorie you consume.

The foundation is simple: eliminate what depletes (sugar, processed foods, seed oils)[5] and prioritize what nourishes (whole foods, especially dark leafy greens). Food should build your body, not break it down.

Reality check: Sometimes you'll have a layover and have to eat airport food, and that's fine. This isn't about perfection or orthorexia. It's about generally trending in the right direction while being human. It's to fuel your body in a way that supports the life you're trying to build.

Movement: The Ultimate Multiplier

Regular exercise slashes mortality by 35% and reduces risks of cardiovascular disease (35%), diabetes (42%), cancer (20-30%), dementia (30%), and depression (26%).[7]

It's not just about fitness. It sharpens your mind, boosts your mood, and enhances your physical appearance from the inside out.[8]

Find movement you enjoy. Dancing, hiking, swimming, lifting, yoga, martial arts—whatever keeps you coming back. When movement becomes joy, consistency follows.[9]

And don't sleep on walking. It's one of the simplest, most underrated practices for boosting mental clarity, mood, fat-loss, and overall health. Aim for 12-15K steps a day.

Antifragility: Strength Through Challenge

In *The Comfort Crisis*, Michael Easter makes a provocative case: we have engineered discomfort out of every corner of modern life — climate control, packaged food, endless entertainment — and in doing so, we may have engineered out the very conditions that make us resilient.[26]

But this relentless avoidance of discomfort is making us fragile. As Nassim Taleb's concept of antifragility[10] highlights: Humans don't just withstand stress, we grow stronger through it.[11]

The antidote is intentional exposure: Lifting weights, fasting, cold plunges, heat exposure, having difficult conversations, and solving complex problems. Each manageable stressor builds resilience that transfers to every area of life.

Intermittent fasting triggers metabolic optimization and cellular repair, improving insulin sensitivity (31%),[22] autophagy (300%),[23] and reducing inflammation (30-40%).[24] I like the 16:8 method.

Heat exposure like saunas, or simply sweating in warm weather strengthens cardiovascular health and triggers protective heat shock proteins. Regular sauna use slashes mortality (40%), heart disease death (50%), and dementia risk (65-66%).[12,13]

Cold therapy such as cold showers, ice baths, or winter walks spikes dopamine (250%) and norepinephrine (530%), reducing inflammation and depression by ~30%, while building mental toughness.[14]

The paradox is powerful: These practices leave you simultaneously relaxed and energized, calm yet alert.

The point isn't to seek suffering—it's to recognize that avoiding all discomfort makes you weak, while intentional challenges make you antifragile. If you can stay calm in ice-cold water, you can stay calm anywhere.

Beyond physical health, your nervous system also needs protection from the constant assault of modern life.

Consciousness: Curate Your Ecosystem

Proximity is not passive. What you allow into your space — people, content, conversations, environments — determines the quality of your energy, thoughts, and ultimately, your life.

Feed Your Mind Intentionally

Your brain doesn't distinguish between watching fear-based content and living it. If you're marinating in the news cycle, horror movies, gossip, or low-vibe energy; it feels real to your nervous system.

Your reticular activating system (RAS)—your brain's filter for what's important pulls in more of what you focus on. Feed it fear and scarcity? It'll highlight more problems. Feed it abundance and gratitude? It'll spot more opportunities.

Be selective with media. If it's not aligned with who you want to become, it doesn't belong in your content diet.

Design your environment. Surround yourself with beauty, opulence, and peace—your nervous system will normalize it as your new baseline.

Choose your conversations. Research shows gossip, complaining, and negativity are contagious. So are inspiration, possibility, gratitude, and expanders.[16]

Raise your average. Jim Rohn's principle, "You become the average of the 5 people you spend the most time with" isn't metaphor; it's neuroscience. Mirror neurons in your brain mimic the emotions, actions, and attitudes of those around you.[16] This even applies to your health. If a close friend becomes obese, your risk rises by 57%, because the people around you are constantly and silently setting the norms your behavior follows.[25]

Select your thoughts. The voice in your head architects your reality, shaping your biology, your confidence, and the actions you take. You don't have to accept the thoughts that arrive; just choose the ones you give a home to.

Even Your Cells Are Listening

Dr. Bruce Lipton discovered our thoughts program our biology. Through epigenetics, he revealed that genes aren't fate; they're switches that flip on or off depending on signals from our environment, emotions, and thoughts.[19]

You inherited your DNA but are not imprisoned by it. In every moment, you're actively participating in its expression.

Harvard psychologist Ellen Langer's research echoes this. In one of her famous studies, elderly men were placed in a re-created 1959 environment for just one week — surrounded by the music, news, and cultural cues of their younger years.

At the end of the week, they showed improved hearing, sharper memory, increased flexibility, and even looked younger in photographs.[21,22] Nothing changed in their bodies except what they believed. That was enough.

Decades of psychoneuroimmunology research has since confirmed it: The mind and body are not separate — they are one deeply integrated system. What happens in your inner world has a direct biological address.

Your immune function, hormonal balance, and cellular repair mechanisms are all downstream of what's happening in your mind.

Every thought you think, your cells are listening. Chronic stress, self-criticism, and shame don't just feel bad — they have measurable biological consequences. And so does their opposite.

Positive self-talk isn't fluffy; it's foundational. You're not just managing your mood, you're programming your biology. Be sure the program supports your flourishing.

Relational Alignment

As you align with your True Self, your tolerance for misalignment drops dramatically. What you once accepted (chaotic environments, draining relationships, toxic dynamics) suddenly becomes intolerable.

You're not becoming "sensitive" or "judgmental." You're becoming attuned. Your nervous system is recalibrating to recognize what actually serves you versus what depletes.

You'll find conversations that once seemed normal now feel exhausting. Relationships you tolerated now feel suffocating. This discomfort is information, not a problem.

Your soul is waking up and refusing to pretend anymore. It's saying: *This isn't okay. It was never okay. I'm just finally awake enough to notice.* You're not being difficult. You're being discerning.

Since turning 40, I've become almost allergic to misalignment. I started saying no unapologetically to invites that wouldn't let me stay aligned, stopped responding to certain texts, and walking away from extractive business relationships.

Trust this sharpening of your boundaries. You can love people from a distance. You can wish others well without exposing yourself to their chaos. You can be compassionate without being consumed.

As you rise, the standards for who and what gets access to your inner world rise with you. This isn't arrogance; it's necessary self-preservation.

If you give your lifeforce to energy vampires and drama, there will be none left for you and the people who deserve it.

How to Identify Aligned Relationships:

- Shared values: Your core values align.

- Mutual growth: You celebrate your wins without jealousy and show up when each other fails.

- Kind candor: You tell each other the truth, even when it's hard. You refuse to cosign on playing small, victim narratives, or self-deception.

Be a Boundary Boss

As psychotherapist Terri Cole says, boundaries teach people how to treat you. By clearly communicating your expectations and being willing to enforce them, you shape the texture of your relationships.

A boundary isn't something you tell others not to do. A boundary is stating what *you* will do if someone crosses your limit.[17] For example: "If you continue to contact me outside of business hours for non-emergencies, I won't respond until the next working day, because protecting that boundary is how I show up fully when it matters."

You can't control others' behavior. But you can control who gets access to you—physically, mentally, and energetically.

How to tell where you need boundaries: Ask where you feel resentful. Resentment means you're over-functioning and need to set or enforce a boundary there.

What Happens When You Start Setting Boundaries

- You'll set a boundary and then violate it yourself within 24 hours.

- People who benefited from your lack of boundaries will suddenly have opinions about your "attitude."

- You'll wonder if you're being too harsh, too selfish, too much. You're not.

- You'll have to set the same boundary multiple times before it sticks.

This is normal. This is the work. Keep going.

So, now you've learned to fill your cup first and build your foundation. Now comes the pushback.

Your ego will protest because authenticity threatens the safety it built through conformity. Others will grow uncomfortable because your transformation mirrors their own self-abandonment. You'll feel tempted to shrink, to second-guess, to make yourself smaller so others can digest you more easily.

Don't. Resistance isn't a red flag; it's a trail marker pointing you forward.

But to keep walking, you need something unshakeable beneath you. You need sovereignty: The return to self-authority, the reclamation of power from the places you've outsourced it.

The next chapter is about taking that power back.

Chapter 10

Be the CEO of Your Life

The Nod That Doesn't Help Anyone

Taylor spent fifteen years building a career that looked, from the outside, like everything he'd ever wanted. He was a senior VP at a respected firm, the kind of title his parents mentioned at dinner parties with quiet pride.

He was sitting in an emergency board meeting, called because the company's largest client was threatening to walk, when something inside him cracked.

The CEO was laying out a response strategy that Taylor knew was catastrophic. Not wrong in a subtle, debatable way. Wrong in a way that would cost the company its most important relationship and put hundreds of jobs at risk.

Taylor had spent 6 months embedded with this client. He understood their frustrations better than anyone in that room. He had a counterproposal that could save the account. He had the data on the laptop in front of him.

The CEO finished speaking. The room nodded. He looked directly at Taylor and asked, "You've been closest to this. What do you think?" Every head turned.

This was Taylor's moment. The account, the jobs, the future of the division — it was all right there.

He opened his mouth and heard himself say, "I think you've got the right approach." Seven words. Fluent, polished, and completely dishonest.

He watched the CEO smile and move on. The room exhaled and he felt something inside him go quiet...dead.

Three months later, the client left. The layoffs came shortly after. forty-seven people lost their jobs. Taylor kept his.

Sitting in his office, knowing he'd had the answer and swallowed it to keep the room comfortable was eating him up.

That was the night Taylor began the terrifying, liberating work of reclaiming his own authority. and not because he'd had an awakening.

Because he'd finally seen, with unbearable clarity, that his silence wasn't just costing him. It was costing everyone around him.

And he decided he was not willing to pay that price ever again.

Reclaim Your Authority

For centuries, we've outsourced our authority to external institutions, religious leaders, governments, corporations, cultural norms, and "experts".

We were taught that truth lives "out there", in the hands of those with titles, credentials, or positions of power.

But now, particularly as we watch these structures crumble, we're waking up to see that authority doesn't equal truth. The real authority on your life is you.

Your Direct Access to Truth

In 1945, a remarkable discovery emerged from the Egyptian desert: a collection of ancient texts so threatening to institutional authority and the patriarchy, that the early church did everything to eliminate them.[1]

These suppressed writings—the Gnostic Gospels, including the Gospels of Mary, Thomas, and Philip—present a revolutionary idea that the institutional church found intolerable: Spiritual truth is accessed through direct, unmediated experience.[2]

Not granted by institutions, earned through suffering or obedience to religious authorities. Not requiring any intermediary between you and the divine. But discovered within, through gnosis; direct experiential knowledge.

The word "Gnostic" comes from the Greek gnōsis, meaning knowledge—but not intellectual knowledge. This is intimate, experiential knowing—the difference between reading about an ocean and diving into one.

Why were these texts suppressed? Because they threatened the entire power structure of organized religion.

If people could access divine truth directly—if salvation came through personal experience rather than institutional mediation—what need would there be for the church?

In the Gospel of Thomas[14] for example, Jesus doesn't preach blind obedience to external authority. He says, "The kingdom of God is inside you and all around you."

This is the language of direct access. No gatekeepers. No middlemen. No external permission required.

The Gospel of Mary (Mary Magdalene) goes further, suggesting that she received teachings directly from Jesus that the male disciples didn't understand—that inner vision and spiritual authority aren't determined by gender, institutional position, or external validation, but by one's capacity for direct experience of the divine.[15]

The institutional response was brutal, declaring Gnostic teachings heretical because they challenged the church's authority, promoted decentralized spirituality, and gave women equal roles.[3]

Communities were persecuted and books were burned.

For nearly 1,600 years, the understanding that each person has direct access to divine truth, was almost entirely erased from Western consciousness.

Until 1945, when an Egyptian farmer digging for fertilizer discovered a sealed jar in the desert, containing these ancient texts perfectly preserved.[4]

This Pattern Plays Out Everywhere

Those in power claim exclusive access to truth, then sell you salvation through their system:

- **The medical complex** tells us, "You need our expertise and our drugs, over trusting your own body's wisdom."

- **The educational system** says, "You can't learn your own way. You need a standardized curriculum and our credentials."

- **Advertising and media** tell us "you're not enough". "You have a problem (you didn't even know you had), and our product is the solution that will make you happy/successful/attractive/complete".

- **Societal conditioning** says, "You can't trust your knowing. You need our approval."

The Gnostic tradition reminds us of what the powers-that-be have always feared: You have direct access. To truth. To wisdom. To your own knowing.

The experts can inform you. Teachers can guide you. Institutions can offer frameworks. But you are the one who has to live with your choices.

This isn't about rejecting all outside information. It's about recognizing that the final authority on your life is you. Not your parents. Not your boss. Not society. Not the algorithm. Not the "experts." You are.

You're the one whose inner knowing has been whispering all along, even when you ignored it to please others.

Sovereignty is the return to that inner knowing. The recognition that you have everything you need inside you. Not because you're perfect or all-knowing, but because you're the only one who can feel what's true for your soul.

No one else has access to that information. Taking your power back isn't arrogant or dismissive. It means becoming the final arbiter of what's true for you.

The Core: Unshakable Self-Worth

Self-worth is the bedrock of everything we're building. Without it, sovereignty is impossible.

If you don't believe you're inherently valuable, you'll subconsciously sabotage yourself. You'll abandon yourself to secure external validation. You'll tolerate mistreatment because you don't believe you deserve better. You'll chase goals that don't align with you because you're trying to prove you're enough.[5]

What Self-Worth Actually Is

Self-worth isn't earned through achievement, appearance, or approval. It's the unshakeable knowing that you matter simply because you exist.

Most of us were never taught this. Instead, we learned conditional worth: "You're valuable when you're good, successful, useful, pleasant, accomplished, attractive."

We internalized the message that worth must be earned and perpetually proven. So we spend our lives chasing achievement, approval, and perfection, trying to finally feel worthy. But the finish line keeps moving because worth was never conditional to begin with.

When you ground yourself in unconditional self-worth, everything changes.

You stop contorting yourself to earn love. You stop tolerating mistreatment. You make decisions based on what's right for you. You set boundaries without guilt. You take bigger risks because rejection doesn't kill you.

How to Cultivate It

Build it through consistent actions that prove you matter:

1. Separate your value from your performance. Notice when you tie your worth to external outcomes—the promotion, relationship status, approval from someone whose opinion you've elevated above your own.

When you catch yourself, pause and ask: *If I had none of these things, would I still matter? Would I still be worthy of love, respect, and dignity?* The answer is always yes.

2. Keep promises to yourself. Every time you follow through on a commitment to yourself—even tiny ones like going to bed on time or protecting an hour for the gym—you send your nervous system a message: *I matter. My needs are important. I'm worth showing up for. I follow through on my commitments.*

Every broken promise reinforces the opposite. This isn't about big, dramatic promises. It's about the small ones that become your character.

When you consistently choose alignment over avoidance, growth over comfort, and truth over ego-protection, you build trust with yourself. You realize you can rely on you.

Real confidence doesn't come from affirmations or achievements. It comes from proof that you're capable of doing difficult things and you can count on yourself.

3. Have your own back. Having your own back means becoming fiercely loyal to yourself; in recognition that you cannot pour from an empty vessel. Your relationship with you sets the tone for everything else. This means:

- Learning to say no without guilt

- Prioritizing your wellbeing without justification

- Speaking your truth even when it's uncomfortable

- Leaving situations that consistently diminish you

When you consistently have your own back, something shifts. You stop leaking energy into resentment. You become solid, whole, trustworthy to yourself, then to others.

The relationships that remain after you stop contorting yourself? Those are the ones worth keeping.

Weekly reflection: Spend 10 minutes reviewing your week:

- When did you honor your boundaries this week? Celebrate these.

- When did you abandon yourself? No shame, just data.

- What are you tolerating that you know isn't okay?

Over time, you'll see patterns: The situations where you consistently abandon yourself and the people whose requests trigger automatic compliance. Self-love is built in small, repeated acts of choosing yourself.

4. Stop self-abandoning. Self-abandonment is the most socially acceptable addiction of our time.

Every time you say yes when you mean no, suppress your truth to avoid conflict, or prioritize everyone else's comfort over your own integrity — you betray yourself. And the cost compounds daily.

It hides everywhere, dressed up as virtue:

- **The chronic people-pleaser** says yes to everything, not from generosity but from an inability to disappoint. We call this "nice" but it's self-betrayal on repeat.

- **The undervalued employee** won't negotiate their salary to avoid discomfort, then resents their employer for a situation they never challenged.

- **The martyred parent** erases themselves in service of their children — abandoning hobbies, friendships, health, and identity — and calls it love. But martyrdom doesn't model devotion. It teaches children that self-neglect is noble.

Each time you sell yourself out, you lose ground. The resentment builds. The vitality dims. You become hollowed out beneath a pleasant surface.

It's death by a thousand paper cuts to the soul.

People who self-abandon believe they're doing others a favor. They're not.

When you consistently sacrifice your wellbeing for someone else's comfort, the resentment always leaks out through passive-aggression, withdrawal, or eventual explosions.

On the receiving end, this feels like being lied to. Because it is. You said yes when you meant no. You swallowed your truth. Then you made them pay for it sideways.

Self-abandonment doesn't protect relationships. It poisons them. Real connection requires honesty, boundaries, and the courage to show up as you actually are.

When you have your own back, you give others the gift of knowing exactly where they stand with you. That's not selfish. That's integrity. Try these:

Take the resentment audit. Resentment is the smoking gun of self-abandonment, your soul's alarm system signaling you've betrayed yourself.[6]

1.Set aside 20 minutes and ask yourself: Where am I feeling resentful right now?

2. Write down every situation, person, or commitment that triggers resentment. Don't edit or justify. Just list.

3. Next, ask: What boundary did I fail to set or honor in each situation. For each one, complete this sentence: "Next time, I'll honor myself by_________."

4. Then pick one boundary to set this week. Just one. Start there.

Adopt the 24-hour rule. Self-abandonment often happens in the pressure of the moment. Someone asks for something, and before you've checked in with yourself, you've already said yes.

Try this simple rule: Give yourself 24 hours before committing to anything that requires your time, energy, or resources. Simply say, "Let me check my calendar and get back to you."

During that window, ask:

- Do I actually want to do this, or am I avoiding disappointing someone?

- Do I have the bandwidth without depleting myself?

- Is this aligned with my values and priorities?

When you respond, be clear: "I appreciate you thinking of me, but I'm not able to take this on right now." No elaborate justifications. No apologies.

The Cost of Becoming

A few years ago, I lost a friendship I'd had for over a decade.

The more I reclaimed my sovereignty — setting boundaries, saying no without justification, refusing to perform the version of myself she was comfortable with — the more our dynamic shifted. And she hated it.

At first, I bent. I softened my boundaries. I made myself smaller to preserve the friendship. Classic self-abandonment dressed up as loyalty.

But the more I contorted, the more resentful I became. Eventually, I had to choose: Her comfort or my integrity.

I chose integrity. The friendship ended. I grieved it like a death — not just of the relationship, but of the version of me who thought she had to shrink to be loved.

Some relationships are built on who you used to be, not who you're becoming.

When you change, some people won't — or can't — come with you. They're not wrong and neither are you. You're just walking different paths now.

The cost is real. And it's still worth paying.

Because the alternative — abandoning yourself to maintain connections that require you to be less than you are — is a slow death of the soul.

Radical Responsibility

You've reclaimed your authority. You've built self-worth. You've stopped abandoning yourself. Now it's time to fully own your power—to take radical responsibility for your life.

Own Your Experience

Jocko Willink calls it extreme ownership. Psychologists call it an internal locus of control.

The bottom line: No one is coming to save you, and the quality of your life depends on how much ownership you take of it.[8]

People with a strong internal locus of control believe their actions and choices meaningfully shape their outcomes. These people consistently report higher wellbeing, greater resilience, stronger achievement, and lower rates of depression and anxiety.

They don't need perfect circumstances to feel capable. They've located the source of their power inside themselves, rather than in the hands of fate, luck, or other people.[16]

Radical responsibility means fully owning your experience; your mindset, your choices, your reactions, your results. It's the shift from victim to architect, from "this is happening to me" to "I'm choosing something different."

Yes, terrible things happen. Yes, the world is chaotic and unjust. Yes, some people start with enormous advantages, while others face systemic barriers. But you're still behind the wheel.

You can't control what happens to you, but you can control how you interpret it, respond, and what you choose next. That's where your power lives.

Viktor Frankl, who survived Nazi concentration camps, understood this: "Everything can be taken from a man but one thing: The last of the human freedoms—to choose one's attitude in any given set of circumstances."

When you take radical responsibility, you stop waiting for the world to change and stop blaming your circumstances, because blaming them keeps you powerless.

The moment you take full responsibility, you reclaim your power. You created this and can create something different.

Be High Agency

Part of radical responsibility is having high agency; the mindset of people who make things happen rather than wait for things to happen to them.

High-agency people don't wait to be chosen; they choose themselves. They don't wait for perfect conditions; they move with what they've got, seeing obstacles as puzzles to solve.

They have an almost irrational bias toward action. They believe solutions exist even when they're not obvious. They operate from the assumption that if something needs to change, they can figure out how to make it happen.

Just look at Mel, Howard, and Brooke.

Mel Robbins hit rock bottom at 41, unemployed, drowning in debt. Instead of surrendering, she created the "5 Second Rule," which became a viral TEDx talk and bestselling book, followed by the bestselling book "Let Them," and a top podcast reaching tens of millions. She stopped hiding from creditors and started teaching millions how to take control of their lives.[9]

Howard Schultz grew up in public housing with no safety net and no roadmap. After joining Starbucks and becoming obsessed with bringing Italian espresso culture to America, the founders refused to expand. So he left, and pitched over 200 investors before raising the money to start his own coffee company. Later, he bought Starbucks and transformed 6 stores into a global empire worth over $100 billion. He didn't wait to be chosen. He chose himself.[10]

Dr. Brooke Goldner was diagnosed with lupus at 16. By her twenties, her kidneys were failing. She refused to accept it, discovered that hyper-nutrition (green juices and smoothies) could reverse her disease, and went into complete remission. Now, decades later, she teaches thousands to do the same.[11]

Break Free From Limiting Beliefs

As Abraham Maslow observed, we are "just as afraid of becoming better as we are of becoming worse." The Jonah Complex — the fear of one's own greatness — shows up in predictable ways: Self-sabotaging at the threshold of success, shrinking in the presence of others, fearing the consequences of your own power. These fears feel protective. They're actually prison walls.[12]

In a classic experiment, fleas in a jar with a lid learned to jump just below its height. When the lid was removed, they continued jumping to the same limited height — free to escape but unable to see it. Even later generations born in a lidless jar inherited the same invisible ceiling.[13]

That voice telling you to stay small isn't truth. It's a very old program — written in childhood, when expressing yourself felt dangerous; reinforced by families where success triggered jealousy; and hardened in relationships where your growth reminded others of their own unlived lives.

You're still dimming your light because someone, once told you it was too bright. Stop living within limits that no longer exist.

Don't let fear keep you small. The world needs you fully expressed.

The Sovereign Life

Sovereignty is the radical act of becoming the author of your own life — rather than a character in someone else's story. It's what remains when you stop outsourcing your identity to the opinions and expectations of others. And it begins the moment you realize that the permission you've been waiting for was never theirs to give.

Sovereignty isn't a destination. It's a practice—a daily return to self-authority in a world constantly asking you to outsource your power.

Some days you'll nail it. You'll set the boundary, speak the truth, and choose yourself without flinching. Other days you'll slip back into old patterns—you'll say yes when you mean no. You'll shrink to make someone comfortable. You'll abandon yourself to keep the peace. Both are part of the path.

What matters is that you notice. That you course-correct. That you keep coming back to the question: *Am I honoring myself right now, or am I performing for approval?*

This is the work. It's not dramatic. It's not Instagram post-worthy. Just the consistent, courageous choice to have your own back. Again. And again. And again.

Until one day, you look back and realize: You're not performing your life anymore. You're living it. Your worth isn't up for debate. It simply is.

You're not waiting for permission. You're the authority on your own life. The opinion that matters most is your own.

The Cost and the Reward

Let me be honest about what sovereignty requires.

You will disappoint people. You will be misunderstood. You will lose relationships that cannot survive your expansion.

People who benefited from your smallness will resist your growth. They may call you selfish and accuse you of changing.

They're right; you are changing. You're becoming who you actually are instead of who they needed you to be.

And yes, that's uncomfortable—for them and for you.

But here's what you gain:

- **You get yourself back.** The you that's been buried under expectations, conditioning, and performance. The you that knows what it wants, what it needs, what it will no longer tolerate.

- **You get energy.** Because you're no longer hemorrhaging lifeforce into self-betrayal and resentment. You get to direct that power toward what actually matters.

- **You get real relationships.** Not based on your performance or usefulness, but on mutual respect and genuine connection. The people who stay after you stop contorting yourself? They're your people.

- **You get agency.** The deep knowing that you can trust yourself, you're capable of hard things, and you have your own back.

Sovereignty Within Systems

Most people spend their lives embedded in institutions that prioritize conformity over individuality.

Sometimes, you can't just opt out. Here's how you maintain sovereignty within systems that weren't designed for it:

Internal sovereignty is the foundation — the one thing no institution can control. Separate your identity from your role, maintain your own values, and when they tell you stories like "you're not leadership material" or "you're too sensitive," ask: *Is this true, or is this designed to make me more controllable?*

Behavioral sovereignty means creating pockets of authentic action within constraints. Set micro-boundaries: No email after 7 p.m., or "let me think about that" instead of an automatic yes. Be fully yourself in some contexts, more strategic in others. Small acts of agency remind you that compliance isn't total.

Structural sovereignty is the long game. Can you maintain integrity here? If not, what's your exit plan? Are you building leverage (skills, savings) for future freedom? Sometimes sovereignty means choosing to stay, clearly and deliberately, eyes wide open, while maintaining your essential self.

Your Next Move

You've done the work in this chapter. You understand the principles. But understanding doesn't create change; action does. Identify one area where you've been outsourcing your authority.

Maybe it's:

- Waiting for someone's approval before deciding

- Tolerating a relationship that diminishes you

- Staying silent when you have something to say

- Abandoning your needs to keep the peace

Pick one. Just one. Then ask yourself: *What would it look like to reclaim my power here?*

Maybe it's having the conversation you've been avoiding, or setting the boundary, making the decision, or simply saying no without an explanation or apology.

Whatever it is, do it this week. Not perfectly. Not flawlessly. Just courageously.

Because sovereignty isn't built in grand gestures. It's built in small acts of self-loyalty that accumulate into an unshakeable foundation.

You are the authority on your life. Not because you're perfect or all-knowing, but because you're the only one living it.

Trust yourself.

Have your own back.

Choose you.

The world doesn't need another people-pleaser. It needs you—fully expressed, authentic, and powerfully sovereign.

Chapter 11

What Success Looks Like When It's Yours

The Deathbed Question

Most people spend their one life living someone else's story.[1] We know this because 92% of people say so — on their deathbeds, when it's too late to change it.[2]

Bronnie Ware spent years listening to people in their final days. As a palliative care nurse, she had a front-row seat to humanity's last moments—the space where all pretense falls away and only truth remains.

She discovered the most common regret wasn't about mistakes made or risks taken. It was about lives unlived.

People mourned not living life on their own terms—failing to express their true selves, their deepest desires, their authentic voice.

They didn't regret the promotion they didn't get. They regretted spending decades chasing promotions that didn't actually matter to them.

They didn't regret the relationship that ended. They regretted staying in relationships that were dead for years because they were afraid to disappoint people.

They didn't regret trying something and failing. They regretted never trying at all.

There will come a day when your time here ends. And when that day arrives, you won't be thinking about what people thought of you, the accolades you received, or the external validation you sought. You'll be asking yourself: *Did I really live? Did I follow my soul's whisper? Did I show up as the real me? Did I give everything I had?*

This isn't morbid contemplation; it's liberation. When we truly grasp the finite nature of our existence, we begin to live with an urgency that cuts through the noise of societal expectations and awakens us to what truly matters.

So let me ask you: What does success actually mean to you? Not what your parents wanted, what looks impressive on LinkedIn, or what your peers are chasing. What does success mean to your soul? This bar is the only one that matters.

An Inner Vs. Outer Scorecard

Warren Buffett once said the biggest factor in how people behave is whether they run on an inner or outer scorecard — and that it helps to be satisfied with the inner one. Most people never realize they have a choice.

An outer scorecard means measuring your worth by others' approval, comparison, and society's milestones — and it guarantees you'll never feel like enough. The bar keeps moving. It was never yours to begin with.

An inner scorecard means you define your own metrics and measure your life by whether you're living according to your values and showing up with integrity, regardless of who's watching, applauding, or keeping score.

To stop running on someone else's scorecard, strip away the external metrics — income, title, approval, status — and ask: "How would I know I'd lived a good day?" "Did I tell the truth?" "Was I present?" "Did I choose courage over comfort?" That's the only score that matters.

The Outsider Advantage

For as long as I can remember, I've lived by my own scorecard. Maybe it comes from standing at the edges of different worlds, never fully belonging to any of them.

I grew up in a chaotic blue-collar house where I never quite fit, but went to school with kids from wealthy, stable families with calm homes and clear futures laid out.

I admired what they had, but I had something better: Freedom. When you don't fit into anyone's box, you build your own. When there's no blueprint, you become one.

Looking back, I realize the key was developing such a solid sense of self that I could feel at home anywhere. I moved between worlds, connecting genuinely, without being bound by the rules of any single one. I made myself the foundation and shaped my life around that, rather than twisting myself to fit someone else's expectations.

This pattern shows up repeatedly among people who've changed the world: Jeff Bezos, Elon Musk, Oprah Winfrey, Howard Schultz, and Tony Robbins. Many share similar origin stories—immigrant experience, troubled upbringing, neurodivergence, poverty, not fitting in.[5,6]

What society deems a disadvantage becomes the key out of the cage of expectations. When you're already on the outside, you're not trying to get back in. You have nothing to lose—you're free to build something entirely new.

If you've ever felt like an outsider, it's not a weakness; it's your edge. The very thing that made you feel different is what frees you from needing everyone's approval. You don't have to wait for permission to live on your terms.

When you're not waiting on validation, you're free to take risks—big, bold, beautiful risks. You can lead, disrupt, create, and transform because it's true to you.

What True Success Looks Like

Society has clear definitions of success: Wealth, status, titles, possessions, followers, influence. These aren't wrong; they're just insufficient.

For many people, these are misaligned with what makes them genuinely fulfilled. The question isn't whether those things matter. The question is: Do they matter to *you*? And if so, *why*?

One of the most common pitfalls is chasing wealth reflexively. I get it; when you're living paycheck to paycheck, money colonizes your entire mental space. But as Daniel Kahneman has shown, once your basic needs are met, nothing outside you will fill the hole inside.[7]

Money cannot purchase fulfillment.[8] What it *can* do is buy freedom—the ability to walk away from harmful jobs, toxic people, and degrading situations. It's leverage. Make it work for you rather than becoming its slave.

Research shows real fulfillment comes from 3 areas:

1. Meaningful work: Work that uses your gifts, aligns with your values, and contributes something that matters to you. You don't have to change the world, you just have to do something that feels meaningful to your soul.

A 2023 McKinsey study found that employees who find their work meaningful are 69% less likely to quit and have twice the job satisfaction.[9] More importantly, they show significantly lower rates of depression and anxiety, regardless of salary.

Psychologist Amy Wrzesniewski's research at Yale revealed meaning has nothing to do with occupation type. Even janitors who saw their work as a calling were more fulfilled than lawyers who viewed theirs as just a job.[10,11]

2. Authentic relationships: Connections where you can be fully yourself without performance or pretense. Relationships built on mutual respect, shared values, and genuine care.

Harvard's longest-running study on happiness found the strongest predictor of well-being, health, and longevity is the quality of your relationships.[12,13] People with strong social connections live longer, experience less cognitive decline, and report significantly higher life satisfaction.

But here's the key: It's about quality over quantity. One deeply authentic friendship where you can be 100% yourself is worth more than fifty superficial connections.

3. Aligned lifestyle: A life that honors your needs, reflects your values, and allows you to be who you truly are—this mean how you spend your time, where you live, who surrounds you, and the rhythms that govern your days.

Research on "value-behavior consistency" shows people living in alignment with their values report 3x higher life satisfaction than those with value-behavior gaps.[14] Even small misalignments accumulate into chronic dissatisfaction and "existential regret."[15]

Research shows how you spend your time matters more than what you achieve. People whose days focus on meaningful activities have higher well-being than those pursuing "successful" but misaligned ones.[16]

Lifestyle alignment isn't about what looks impressive; it's whether your daily reality reflects who you actually are.

How Success Evolves Through Life

Success isn't static. We live in seasons; not straight lines. Each season asks something of us; some are for building, stretching, and sprinting. Others for rest or reorienting. If we don't account for these cycles, we end up chasing outdated goals or holding ourselves to standards that no longer fit who we're becoming.

Understanding Your Personal Seasons

Life doesn't unfold on a universal timeline. Your circumstances, choices, and challenges create a unique rhythm that may not map neatly to traditional phases.

My seasons have been atypical. I was an adult when I was young—hyper responsible, working relentlessly to transcend my circumstances, focused entirely on building and achieving. I never learned how to relax or play.

As an adult, I've had to actively teach myself how to do things purely for enjoyment and take time off without guilt. I'm living a season most people experience decades earlier, but it's exactly what my life is asking of me now.

Your seasons are shaped by your specific circumstances.

For example:

- **If you had kids young:** Your 30s and 40s might look radically different from someone who had them later or not at all.

- **If you faced early adversity:** You might have been forced into grind mode before you had time to explore. Now you're circling back to experimentation and play in your 40s or 50s.

- **If you changed careers mid-life:** You might be in "building" season at 50, while others are in "integration" season.

The point isn't to force yourself into the "right" season for your age. It's to recognize what season you're actually in and honor what it's asking of you.

Identify Your Current Season

To figure out what season you're in, look for these signals:

- **Your energy.** Do you feel pulled to create and push forward, or to simplify and recalibrate?

- **Your inner questions.** Are you asking "What's next?" (building) "What matters?" (contribution) or "What needs to change?" (transition)

- **Your constraints.** What realities—family, health, career, finances—are shaping this chapter?

- **Your longings.** What do you secretly wish you could spend more time on? What feels overdue? What is this season asking of you?

Your Personal Success Definition

Now it's time to get specific. Complete these sentences:

- Success for ME means:

- I know I'm successful when:

- The life I'm building is one where:

- I want to be remembered for:

- When I'm 80, I'll consider my life well-lived if:

Write this down. Put it somewhere you'll see it. Return to it quarterly and ask: *Am I living according to this, or have I drifted back into society's script?*

What's Next

You've done the deep work. You know what matters. You've reclaimed your authority, built your self-worth, and defined success on your own terms.

Now comes the part that separates those who transform from those who just consume content: Living it.

Because knowing your truth and living it are different battles entirely.

The moment you claim what's real for you, every force in your life — external and internal — will push back.

Old patterns will reassert themselves. People who benefited from your compliance will resist your change. Your own nervous system will lobby for the familiar.

That's where daily practice comes in — the unglamorous, consistent work of closing the gap between who you know yourself to be and how you actually show up.

This is where most people quit. They read the book, feel the spark, then slide back into the life they were living before the first page.

Not you.

Chapter 12

Living It

Will The Real Guru Please Stand Up

His friends called him "the guru." Not because he meditated or burned incense — because Marcus could diagnose anyone's life with terrifying accuracy.

Over beers, he'd explain exactly why his buddy kept dating narcissists. At dinner parties, he'd casually unpack the attachment theory behind someone's failing marriage. People would stare at him and say, "You should be a therapist." He'd laugh it off.

What they didn't know was Marcus had been in therapy for 4 years, had read more psychology books than most practitioners, and could map his own childhood wounds with the precision of a surgeon marking incision lines.

He knew everything. He knew his people-pleasing came from a father who only showed affection when Marcus performed. He knew his workaholism was a shame response. He knew his inability to say no was destroying his health, and his relationship with his wife and kids.

He knew all of it. He could narrate his own self destruction in real time and still not stop it.

On a Tuesday night, at 11 pm, Marcus pulled up his driveway. He'd just spent 4 hours finishing a presentation for a colleague who'd dumped it on him at 5 pm; the same colleague who did this 3 times before, the one Marcus had told his therapist he was finally going to confront.

His phone lit up. A text from his wife: "The kids waited up for you. They just fell asleep."

Below it, a photo of his 6-year-old daughter curled up on the couch with a book open on her chest, waiting for a father who chose someone else's deadline over her bedtime story.

Marcus sat there, engine off, staring at that photo, and understood something that years of therapy had never quite made him feel: his self-awareness wasn't saving him. It had become a sophisticated excuse for not changing.

This is the trap no one warns you about. We live in a culture that treats self-awareness as the finish line, as though naming the pattern is the same as breaking it. It isn't.

You can journal every morning, know your enneagram and your attachment style and your mother wound, and still betray yourself before lunch. Knowledge without practice is just an articulate version of being stuck.

The real work — the work most people never do — isn't discovering who you are. It's closing the gap between who you know yourself to be and how you actually live, one uncomfortable choice at a time.

That's what this chapter is about. Not more insight. It's time for the integration.

This Is Practice, Not Perfection

You can know your truth and still not live it. You can understand your values and still betray them. You can identify your purpose and still avoid it.

Information without implementation is just entertainment. The gap between knowing and living is where most people quit—and where transformation actually happens.

This entire book has been building toward this moment. Not the moment you understand yourself. The moment you *become* yourself.

Let me tell you what's going to happen next:

You'll have a week where you feel completely aligned. You'll think, "I've got this. I've cracked the code."

Then life will happen: A crisis. A deadline. A family emergency. The kids get sick. And you'll fall out of alignment.

This is not failure. This is being human.

The old you stayed in the spiral for weeks without noticing. The new you notices within days or hours.

Progress isn't measured by how often you fall out of alignment, but how quickly you notice and how gently you return.

Integration is the capacity to:

- Notice when you've drifted (faster than before)

- Course-correct without self-judgment (with compassion, not criticism)

- Shorten the time between falling out and returning (days not months)

Turn On Your Observer

The single most powerful tool for integration is activating your Observer—the part of you that can watch your experience without being consumed by it.

Previously, when something triggered you, you may have *become* the emotion:

- Someone criticized you and you *were* the defensiveness.

- Your partner said something hurtful and you *were* the anger.

- You missed a deadline and you *were* the shame.

When you're identified with the emotion, you have no choice. The emotion runs you.

But what if you could notice: *Ah, defensiveness is here. Anger is showing up. Shame is present.*

How to Activate It

When you can observe your experience instead of being it, you have space. And in that space, you have a choice.

1. The shitstorm pause: The moment you notice a strong emotion, stop and take 3 conscious breaths and ask: "What's happening right now?" *I'm noticing anger, my body's tight.*

Naming what's present, without judgment, creates the space of the Observer.[1] Then choose your response from this more spacious place.

Practice this daily with small irritations like traffic, interruptions, and feedback at work.

2. The balcony view: When triggered, imagine rising above the scene. You're on a balcony, looking down. From there:

- What patterns are you running?

- What are you protecting?

- What are you reacting to?

- What would your wisest self see?

3. The nightly review: Before sleep, replay your day like watching a movie. Notice moments of alignment and misalignment without judgment.

When you see yourself react from old programming, ask yourself: *What was I protecting? What would aligned action have looked like?*

Watch yourself with compassionate curiosity. Not criticizing, just noticing.

After a few weeks, you'll catch yourself mid-pattern: *Oh, there I go again, getting defensive.* This is gold. Once you see the pattern, you can interrupt it.

The Truth About This Work

Let me tell you what I wish someone had told me at the beginning — this work will cost you:

- **Resistance.** the closer you get to your truth, the harder the old patterns fight back. They don't go quietly.

- **Responsibility.** when you claim your power, you lose the comfort of blaming others.

- **Loneliness.** you'll outgrow relationships that once felt like home.

But you know what's more expensive? Spending your entire life pretending to be someone you're not.

The 30-Day Integration Framework

Most people fail at integration because they try to change everything at once. They read a book, get inspired, and attempt to overhaul their entire life on Monday. By Thursday, they're exhausted and the following Monday, they're back to old patterns.

This framework is different. Instead of transforming overnight, you build gradually—stacking practices that create momentum across everything we've learned.

Week 1: Foundation - Anchor Your Practice

A. Daily Morning Practice

Before you check your phone or do anything else, create space to remember who you are. It could be reading, journaling, movement, or meditation....whatever speaks to you. The point is to start the day on your terms. Same time, same place, every day for 7 days.

B. Daily Evening Reflection

Every evening, review your day:

- What does my True Self need?

- Where am I performing versus being authentic?

- What would more alignment look like?

C. Weekly Sovereignty Check-In

Every Sunday (or day of your choice) review your week:

- Where did I honor myself?

- Where did I abandon myself?

- Which core needs got met? Which got ignored?

Week 2: Awareness - Gather Your Data

A. Continue Your Week 1 Activities

B. Add the Energy Audit

Track your energy through the day:

Time | Activity | Energy Before | Energy After | Drain/Fill?

At the end of the week, look for patterns: What consistently drains you? What consistently fills you? Where are you leaking energy?

C. Add the Values Alignment Check

Rate each major life area below 1-10 for alignment with your core values:

- Work/Career/Business

- Relationships

- Health/Body

- Money/Resources

- Environment/Home

For any area scoring below 7, ask "What would alignment look like?" and "What's one small shift I could make?"

Week 3: Action - Make One Major Shift

A. Continue Your Week 1 Activities

B. Choose One Area To Focus On

Review your Values Alignment Check for the area where misalignment is costing you the most:

- **If work is draining you:** Set a boundary (don't check email after 7 pm).

- **If a relationship requires self abandonment:** Have the difficult conversation.

- **If your mornings feel chaotic:** Redesign your routine to include 30 minutes that belong only to you.

Week 4: Integration - Solidify and Sustain

A. Continue Your Week 1 Activities

B. Evaluate Your Major Shift

Ask, what's working and what adjustments are needed?

C. Lock In Your Systems

- **Daily non-negotiables:** What 3 things must happen daily to feel aligned?

- **Weekly rhythms:** Add your Sovereignty Check-In to your G-cal.

- **Monthly review:** Assess alignment across all three soul needs.

Assess

At the end of every week, ask yourself one question: "Am I living more from my truth today than I was yesterday, last week, last year?"

If yes—celebrate. That's all that matters.

If no—get curious. Without judgment, ask: "What pulled me off course? What do I need to return?"

The Transformation

After you close this book, take a breath and begin.

Tomorrow morning, when your alarm goes off, you have a choice. The old you would hit snooze and reach for your phone. The new you puts your feet on the floor and begins.

These tiny, daily choices are where transformation lives. The quiet, consistent, courageous choice to honor yourself. Again. And again.

Until one day, you look back and realize:

- You're not performing life anymore; you're living it.

- Your values guide your choices consistently.

- Your soul's whisper has become your loudest voice.

Here's what I've learned from walking this path myself and guiding countless others through their own journeys: Reclaiming your life is not a one-time event. It's a daily practice. A moment-by-moment choice.

Some days you'll nail it. Some days you'll face-plant. Both are part of the path. What matters is that you keep walking.

You've spent enough time living someone else's story. Enough time abandoning yourself to keep the peace.

The reclamation begins now.

Not someday.

Not when you're ready.

Now.

Conclusion

The Story That Still Haunts Me

Charlotte spent 78 years being good. A good daughter. A good wife. A good mother. A good friend. A good neighbor.

She said yes when she meant no. She swallowed her dreams to fund everyone else's. She made herself smaller so others could feel bigger.

Three days before she died, her daughter found her sobbing in her hospice bed—deep, guttural sobs that shook her frail body.

"Mom, what's wrong? Are you in pain?"

Charlotte looked at her daughter with an expression that would scar her forever. Not physical pain. Something worse.

"I spent my whole life trying to be who everyone needed me to be," she whispered. "And now it's over, and I never got to be me."

Her daughter Mary told me this story five years later at a coffee shop.

Mary was a successful attorney. Married. Two kids. The picture of having it all together.

She broke down completely. "My mother was beloved," she said through tears. "Everyone at her funeral talked about how selfless she was, how giving, how kind. And all I could think was: She gave everything away. Including herself."

Then she looked at me with wild, desperate eyes. "I'm doing the same thing. I wake up exhausted. I resent my own life. I can't remember the last time I did something just because I wanted to. I'm 45 and I'm disappearing just like she did."

Charlotte and Mary are not outliers. They are the norm.

How many of us are living this exact pattern right now — performing, pleasing, perfecting — convinced that if we just try harder, we'll finally earn the right to be ourselves?

But that day never comes. Because being yourself isn't something you earn. It's something you choose. And every day you postpone that choice, you don't just lose time — you lose yourself, incrementally, quietly, in ways that are hard to name until the loss becomes undeniable.

The life you keep deferring was never waiting on the other side of enough. It was always here. You just kept choosing the performance instead.

The End Of the Old Story

By now, you know the truth.

You know how the world has systematically trained you to live from the outside in—to trust everyone except yourself, to value everything except what actually matters.

You know the cost: The hollowness, the exhaustion, the regret, the sense that you're living someone else's life.

That chapter is over. You can't unsee what you now know.

You've done the deep work. You've excavated your conditioning. You've met your True Self. You've clarified your values. You've discovered your assignments. You know how to feed your soul, fill your cup first, and own your power.

You have everything you need.

The only question now is: Will you use it?

Because knowing it doesn't change anything; living it does.

What to Expect

Let me be honest about what's ahead.

This will be hard. You will probably disappoint people.

You will set boundaries and feel crushing guilt. You will speak your truth and watch someone withdraw. You will choose alignment and lose relationships.

And you will keep going anyway.

Because the cost of staying the same is higher than the cost of changing.

Every time you choose yourself, you're reversing years of conditioning.

The resistance you feel? That's not evidence you're doing it wrong. That's evidence you're doing something your old programming doesn't want you to.

So when the guilt comes, remind yourself: *This is my conditioning protesting change.*

When the fear comes, remind yourself: *This is my ego protecting a version of me that no longer serves.*

When the doubt comes, remind yourself: *This is the voice of a world that benefits from my smallness.*

And then keep going.

Your Assignment

Close this book. Look around at your actual life—not the one you wish you had, but the one you're living right now.

Ask yourself: Does this life honor who I actually am, or does it violate my truth?

Don't sugarcoat it. Don't judge it. Just be honest.

Start with one thing. One boundary. One truth. One choice that honors your soul.

Tomorrow, do it again. And again. Until one day you look around and realize: *This life is mine and I love it.*

I think about Charlotte a lot. About how she waited until it was too late.

Your time is also finite. And it's running out.

Every hour you spend living someone else's script is an hour you will never get back.

So let me ask you: If you keep living the way you're living now, what will you regret when it's your turn to go?

Sit with that question. The answer is your roadmap.

Whatever you'd regret not doing, do it now.

Whatever you'd regret not saying, say it now.

Whatever you'd regret not becoming, become it now.

The life you were meant to live is waiting.

Go claim it.

References

This book draws on extensive research and hundreds of citations.

In honoring my value of environmental stewardship, I've made the complete list of references available online rather than printing 30 additional pages in every book.

Access all references at:

www.tonillemiller.com/ffwreferences.